TO BE A CLOWN

Elizabeth Macdonald

ISBN# 978-1484003695

©1994 By Elizabeth Macdonald

Published by
2B Free Book Company
PO Box 174
Gainesville, GA 30503
www.2bfreebooks.com
contactus@2bfreebooks.com

Dedicated to

Ray Page

the original Addison Ray

Chapter One

Wood's Home

"If I ever get me some loose change, I'm blowin' this joint. Ain't no one gonna make a workhorse outta me. All I need is some sappy-lookin' clothes. I'd show 'em. If I could just get a break."

The leather yoke cut into Addy's shoulder and chest where his tan hide strained against the weight of the straps. A stubborn streak of blond hair batted his eyes at each jolt of his rocky gait. Addy lifted a grimy arm to his forehead to wipe away the sweat, leaving a streak of rich dark earth behind. He winced at the pain in his shoulder. Even though he was big for his age, pulling a harrow was hard work for a twelve-year-old boy.

Wood's Home for Wayward Boys was the only world Addy had ever known. In the year 1924, for reasons unknown to Addy, he had been abandoned at a park in nearby Copperstock. Because Addy was large and contemptuous-looking, couples looking for little boys passed him by. At ten, Addy became a ward of the state and Barley, the owner of the orphanage, was assigned permanent foster care. Barley raised Addy to take care of the fields and manage the other orphans. Addy grew up quickly.

Barley plagued Addy with stories about his parents. How his mother was the "bad kind, unmarried." And how his "drunk old man" had showed up one day to try to adopt Addy, but that when he seen how ugly the kid was, he said he'd "rather die a poor drunk than the father of an ugly mut."

In time, Addy learned not to trust the old man. Barley was selfish, lazy, and dirty. He'd been trading boys for bribes and jobs as long as Addy could remember. Since Addy was strong and obedient, the old man used him to work the fields and look after the other orphans.

"It won't be long 'for I can take him." Addy continued talking as he leaned into his harness. "I'll look him right in the eye and then I'll split open his ugly nose until his eyes roll down his face. When he drops to his knees I'll kick his teeth back to his tonsils. Then I'll leave him there for the buzzards while I break open the till...and the file cabinet." I can't forget the file cabinet. Addy thought the words over in his mind.

At the end of the row, Addy dropped the harness off his shoulder and turned to rest against the wooden shaft. The evening breeze was rolling down from the forested ridge and mixing with the sultry air of the Connecticut valley like cool spring water, bringing with it an end to another dreary day. The narrow road to town fought the breeze and whipped the small gusts of air with its dust.

Bobbing across the road to the fields came three bright balloons, anchored together with string and a bow. Addy stretched and shaded his eyes against the setting sun. How strange, he thought. Where did they come from? A wind devil swirled the balloons and they danced over the tilled rows like swallows, dipping and bumping together as the wind carried them along.

For a moment Addy pictured himself as a clown. He could hear the music of the calliope, the laughter of children, the trumpet in the band, and

6

the cry of an elephant as it pawed the air like a magic giant. Sparkling costumes glittered in the dying sun – the vision was blinding.

"Addison," Barley roared from the farm, "Addison Ray, get your scrawny carcass back here."

The music stopped, the circus disappeared and Addy dropped the harness across the harrow. With one limp wave of recognition, he headed back to Wood's Home.

The circus must be in town, thought Addy to himself. I could get a job as a clown and be in another county before Barley even takes a head count.

"Money," said Addy, "I've got to find some money." The breeze made the sweat on his skin tingle at the thought of leaving the orphanage. Maybe, with some money, it wouldn't be too hard to make it – out there. But if Barley caught him, well, he'd never get a second chance. The timing would have to be just right. The only thing was...it would be hard to leave Skunker.

Just like Addy, Skunker had been at the orphanage since he was a baby; that made them almost brothers. One of these days someone will adopt Skunker though and he'll be a real boy with folks and everything. With dark brown curly hair, eight years of freckles, and an angel-round face, it was only a matter of time before someone snatched him away from Barley's motley group of abandoned boys.

Addy kicked the sun-burnt root of an old oak and looked down the fence line at the orphanage. Not like me, he thought. I'm too big and I ain't a pretty sight like Skunker. My blond hair looks greasy most of the time and people think I'm dangerous, like a mean dog, even though I ain't.

7

Nobody ever even gave me a try. I wouldn't squish a flea; I just talk rough 'cause it keeps Barley off my back. Addy thought these things over to himself as he walked, his shoulders drooping, his hands hooked over the holey pockets of his denim overalls.

"Addy, get over here before I skin your worthless hide," Barley growled from the driveway, choking over a wad of chew.

Exhausted from plowing, Addy dropped his head and jogged the rest of the way to Barley's car.

Chapter Two

Skunker

"The seed's in, so I'm going to town, Addy."
Barley spit into the dirt and wiped his mouth on the
loose-fitting sleeve of his gray coat. "See that the
others get their chores finished. I left the mutton
stewing on the stove."

Addy passed the old man and dragged himself
up the steps to the porch, avoiding Barley's cruel
hawk-eye stare.

"You hear me, son? I said..."

"I heard."

The smell of tobacco chew and old sweat
lingered in the still hot air of the porch. The boy
stood and listened as the man scratched his rough
face. Addy could feel the hard eyes on his back like
the noon sun, until the old man cleared his throat
and stepped away. Barley slammed the door to the
Buick and swore as the car coughed up the energy to
sputter down to the gate.

It didn't help to sigh except to blow away the
stale scent of Barley's breath. With one hand on the
smooth brass knob to the front door, Addy listened
as the wrought iron gate to Wood's Home locked into
place behind the Buick. The whine of the car could
be heard for some time as Barley gunned the
protesting engine all the way down the road.

"Addy, is Barley gone?" came a small squeaky
voice from inside the house.

Behind the door, three small boys waited
patiently for an answer. Addy laughed as he opened

the door. He flicked the crazy red cowlick of one boy and tousled the hair on Skunker's forehead.

"Cut it out, Addy," said Skunker, "I'll bust you into pieces." Arms flailed out and the boys giggled as they made a valiant effort to bring Addy down with an attack at the knees.

"No you won't, Skunker. You're not ready to take me on yet. Besides, you shouldn't try to solve all your problems by bustin' things up. Who's gonna adopt a freckle-faced pit bull?"

The rollicking stopped and the boys ran outside screaming in delight as the "Addy monster" chased them across the porch.

"Get your chores done, you good for nothin' sewer rats," Addy said, trying to scowl like Barley, but as usual it came out with a chuckle.

"You're about as fierce as a mouse, Addy," Skunker said, running backwards to keep up with his friends, but a rock caught his heel and Skunker dropped into the dust.

"And you're graceful too," Addy teased, jumping up to the railing and balancing on one foot. The children turned and cheered as Addy performed for them.

"Look at me," Addy continued, "I'm Addy the Magnificent." Addy grabbed a rag draped across the railing and stretched it tightly between his hands. He jumped over the rag, without breaking his hold. The porch railing quivered under the strain, but Addy regained his balance and bowed. The boys cheered.

Addy snapped the rag and twirled it in the air as he perched like a stork on one leg and used his toes to creep about in a half turn.

"Please," Addy boomed, imitating the roar of a circus ringmaster, "Silence. Addy the Magnificent will now attempt a death-defying leap into mid-air. Yes folks, ten thousand feet above the ground. You will be the first to witness an amazing stunt, never before seen on the face of the Earth."

"Addy, don't," Skunker protested. "You're gonna kill yourself."

As if in preparation for a race, Addy drew his arms up to his sides, pulled his hands into fists, balanced on one foot, and stuck his tongue out comically across one cheek. Then gracefully he cartwheeled along the railing, somersaulted to the porch, cartwheeled again to the far side of the deck and vaulted off the railing into the bushes.

From all over the farm, boys cheered. Skunker ran around to the side of the porch, his big brown eyes milky with concern for his friend.

"Don't do that, Addy."

"Don't worry, Skunker. I was born to be a clown. It's a part of me. I could never hurt myself."

"Addy, you can't never be a clown. Where you gonna get all them fancy clothes and paint and stuff?"

"You don't need nothin' to be a clown. Bein' a clown is like bein' God. Your job is to watch over things and make people happy." Addy looked around at the other children and yelled at them to get back to work. Then he set a heavy tired hand on Skunker's shoulder and knelt down on the ground.

"Skunker, I have to be a clown." Addy thought for a minute. He didn't want to tell his friend about the balloons...that the circus was near...that the desire to leave was stronger than ever. "You'll get adopted. You're little. Who could resist such a cute nose." With a thumb between his fingers, Addy stole Skunker's nose and hid it behind the boy's ear, until it appeared at the other ear and

11

he replaced it with a loud smack of his lips.

"Addy, you won't never leave, will you?"

"Look, kid, we all have to move on sometime. When I go it will be because somethin' wonderful is gonna happen. Same for you. You're gonna be famous someday. Why, I'll bet you open a line of stores clear across the country."

"Skunker's General Store?" the boy asked, his freckles doubling over as he wrinkled his nose.

Addy dusted himself off and shook his head. "Could be.

"That's the excitement of it, Skunker. No one knows until it happens, but there's a plan for all of us. Now, go wash. You stink. You want people to call you Skunker the rest of your life?"

With a flash of his brown eyes, the boy jumped to his feet and knocked Addy off balance with a swift blow to the shoulder.

"You freak," Addy yelled as Skunker sped off behind the house. With a painful groan, Addy straightened and rubbed his shoulder, still burning from the strain of a day's work. His bare toes scraped the dust as he moped wearily to the wash basin at the back of the house.

"Where am I gonna get some cash?" Addy said absent-mindedly, the image of the bouncing balloons still tugging at his heart, calling him to be free.

Chapter Three

The Office

After the orphans were fed, two boys fought
over the clean up while the rest slowly straggled
outside for a game of stick ball. When the kitchen
was done and Addy was alone, he paused in the front
hall to think. Knowing Barley could never resist a
drink, Addy figured he had about an hour before the
old man would return to Wood's Home with the seed.
Why not run away tonight? He had time. Nothing
to carry, nothing to pack. How hard could it be? No
money. It would be tough to run away with no
money, not to mention how bad it would be to get
caught.

Then his eyes settled on the locked door of
Barley's office. There wouldn't be any cash in the
office. Barley was sure to have taken it all to town,
to drink whatever he didn't spend on seed. But
there was the file cabinet. Even if he couldn't leave
yet, he could at least find his file.

Addy walked to the barn and searched the
tools for something strong enough to pry open a lock.
Armed with the largest screwdriver he could find, he
returned cautiously back to the office and tried to
turn the screws on the lock. When that proved
hopeless, he began wedging the screwdriver behind
the plate to push out the screws. The wrought iron
gates clattered and Addy leaped to the window to
watch as the boys retrieved a ball and rattled their
sticks along the fence.

For a moment, Addy surveyed the farm. It

would be easy to go through the fence, he thought to himself. The problem would be to survive on the other side. How long would he last without food or cash? Boys left all the time, but they always came back and each time the punishment was worse. Beatings, isolation, the rough backside of Barley's hand across your face. His rotten breath leaving beads of sweat on your cheek as he held you by the throat and threatened you with more forms of his "proper punishment."

No, thought Addy, when I go, I won't get caught.

After more wiggling and swearing and sweating, the oak splintered beneath the lock and the contraption popped onto the floor. Addy replaced the screws and latch temporarily, leaving the door open just enough to send a crack of light across Barley's desk.

The money box was open. Empty.

Addy opened the top drawer and pocketed two packs of matches and a folded knife. The second drawer had only the stub of a pencil and a pair of dice.

A boy squealed and Addy listened. Since Barley's office had once been a closet, there were no windows, but Addy could hear the boys' feet padding back and forth across the yard, screaming for a chance to bat the rock into a goal. They wouldn't be looking for Addy and they wouldn't leave their game until someone spotted Barley's dust on the road.

From a pile of donated clothes in the corner, Addy could smell the musty odors of other civilizations, houses with food, wood smoke and cats. That was just like Barley to let the clothes rot in his office while the boys ran around half-naked. Addy rummaged through the bundles until he spied a

blazer with brass buttons. A set of rainbow
suspenders caught his eye and he pulled them up
from the bottom along with a huge pair of green
tweed trousers.

"Perfect," he said, glowing with admiration at
his discovery. Addy scrunched up the clothes under
one arm while he inspected the file cabinet.

The slam of a car door echoed across the farm
yard. Addy hadn't noticed that the boys had stopped
playing. He hadn't heard the quiet.

"No," Addy gasped, "not now." Addy used the
wad of clothes to cover his hand as he smashed the
light bulb in the ceiling. There was no hope of
escape – and the front door was already opening,
followed by Barley's heavy drunken shuffle. The
steps thudded across the hall to the office and the
unriveted lock rattled to the floor.

"Thief!" The roar of Barley's discovery shook
the walls of the office as he stormed through the
door. When the light failed, he swore and stumbled
out to the porch. "Call the police! I've been robbed.
Where's Addy. Get over here and line up, you rats."

As Addy crawled out from under the pile of
clothes he could hear the boys running up the steps
of the porch to line up. He could hear Barley yelling,
occasionally smacking the head of an unlucky
orphan who failed to dodge his angry blows.

Addy looked at the file cabinet.

The screwdriver was still on the desk. He
grabbed it to pry open the small lock across the top
drawer. From his pocket he found the pack of
matches and he hurriedly tried to light up the
drawer, but his hands were shaking. On the third
try, a burst of light sparkled long enough for Addy to
fumble through the files until he recognized his
name: ADDISON RAY.

For a moment, Addy held his breath and listened to Barley's heavy boots. The boys were getting a lecture as Barley stormed back and forth across the front porch. He could picture the scowl on the man's face, the belt, doubled over, clenched between his fists, as he paced in front of the boys, a tactic he often used to frighten boys into confession. The belt snapped in Barley's hands. Barley was furious and if Addy stayed, Barley would take his rage out on Addy's backside.

He had to go. Now!

Addy hugged the file and the roll of clothes to his chest as he flew out the office door, across the main hall, to the back of the house, his bare feet a whisper on the wooden floor.

Listening just long enough to assure himself of a few more minutes of Barley's rage, Addy unlatched the door and jumped clear across the back deck to the ground. He ran behind the chicken house, into the paddock around the dairy barn. Moist manure squished between his toes. Addy hopped delicately through the paddock so as not to lose his balance in the slimy dirt.

Once over the rail fence, the coarse pasture grass whipped at his legs. There wasn't time to look back. Every outstretched foot was another step closer to freedom. Addy wasn't stopping. No one was going to catch him...ever.

Chapter Four

Copperstock

Police sirens howled like tom cats along the county road – in the wrong direction. Any respectable bum would have headed for the state line, and that's where the search was directed. Not Addy. He was determined to find the circus, even if it meant dodging recognition in the back streets of Copperstock. He walked until he was exhausted and then crawled inside a patch of laurel to hide.

There were no tears for Addy. It had been a long time since he had cried, although he wanted to. He wasn't happy like he had dreamed he would be. He was afraid of being alone, of going hungry, of dying slowly. He was worried about Skunker and some of the others. He wondered if Skunker was mad or if he'd be crazy enough to run. Maybe Barley had beat the other boys because of him.

"You hurt Skunker and I'll kill you," Addy whispered. He wiped his nose and pulled the blazer over his shoulders as the cold darkness crept in around him. Addy tried to think about the circus. It was the only way he could keep from panicking. He told himself over and over that he would find a job at the circus and never see Barley again.

"I'll be back Skunker. I'll make some money, then I'll come and get you."

Addy squeezed his eyes shut, afraid of what he might see peeking at him from the woods. He listened for sounds from the circus until he finally drifted off to a restless sleep.

At the first light of dawn, Addy shook off the pangs of hunger and trotted through the woods for several hours. He stopped to drink at a stream and set his bundle down while he chewed on a birch twig. Even though it didn't fill the hole in his stomach, it smelled like gum and made him feel better. Then he looked at the file beside him and decided a short rest would do him good.

Withdrawn back between two large boulders, Addy opened the file. For years Addy had been convinced that Barley was right about how lousy his parents were and that they were dead anyway. But, out of cruelty, Barley had slipped one day while teasing him and mentioned the file.

"You're mine," Barley had said, "I named you. You belong to me for the rest of your life and I got the papers to prove it."

Over the miles, the file had become moist and mutilated in his frightened grasp. Addy smoothed out the three pieces of paper. With very little schooling, Addy found the wording confusing. He knew what he wanted the papers to say, but there was little he understood.

The top page was a typed report from the Copperstock Police, dated September 1, 1924:

#2439: Infant boy, abandoned Copperstock Park, discovered 2:20 a.m., admitted Wood's Home 4:30 a.m. for temporary custody until further notice.
Description: Caucasian, brown eyes, blond hair, 12 lbs / 13 oz. approximately 1 month old.

At first, it was a relief to know there was no mention of a mother with the reputation Barley had

18

claimed she had, but then Addy realized there was no real proof either. He turned the page. The second sheet was a heavy piece of paper with gold printing at the top:

District Court in and for the County
of Copperstock in the State of Connecticut

ORDER OF GUARDIANSHIP

In re the custody of A.R. – Juvenile
After considering the State's motion and
supporting brief, the court grants the
State's motion and orders the juvenile A.R.
to be a permanent ward of the State.

Dated this 10 day of June in the year 1934 .

Signed Judge Harold Creaser

The words were hard to understand. So he was "a ward of the State," whatever that meant. At the bottom of the page was a handwritten note: *"Permanent foster care granted to Theodore Wood."* All Addy could figure was that in 1934 the state had handed him over to Barley: "Mr. Theodore Wood." He laughed at the ring of such a fancy name for someone as filthy and cruel as Barley.

One more page. Addy stared at the words, but it looked more like someone had dropped a page into the wrong file. It made no sense at all:

District Court in and for the County
of Copperstock in the State of Connecticut

In re the custody of A.R. – Juvenile

19

*Teodoro Ignacio Lorenzo II is denied custody
due to the lack of documentation supporting
his claim and due to the disappearance of
witness Marie Petrulio Thompson. Hearing
#P313.*

Dated this <u>24</u> day of <u>May</u> in the year <u>1935</u> .

Signed <u>Judge Harold Creaser</u>

The papers were a disappointment. It had
been more fun dreaming of what he had hoped would
be in the file: an address, a picture, an answer to his
prayers. The file said he belonged to Barley, but it
didn't say his parents were dead. Addy decided not
to think of himself as an orphan, but as a clown.

Discouraged, tired, and frightened at the
prospect of being caught and returned to Wood's
Home, Addy folded the file in half and buried it
under some rocks between the two large boulders.
The evidence would probably disintegrate in the
rain, but Addy didn't care. From now on, he was a
young man in search of success, not the property of a
drunken scoundrel who sucked happiness from the
lives of homeless boys in return for a few rotten
bucks.

Within hours, Addy stepped up to the rise
overlooking Copperstock. Circus banners waved a
welcome to him from the city park. The brightly
striped tents sent a rush of warmth through his
body, as if he were arriving home. High hopes
returned and Addy planned his approach. First he'd
find some food, then he'd clean himself up, then he'd
find the boss. Tonight he'd be workin' under the big
top.

In a tight bundle, Addy rolled up his coat,

trousers, and suspenders. He tucked in his shirt and
spit on one palm to slick down his hair.

Chapter Five

The Circus

Skirting the back streets to avoid attention, Addy worked his way through the town of Copperstock. At one small house, a line of laundry billowed in the morning breeze. He looked cautiously around before bounding over the fence to snatch a shirt and a pair of socks. The large trousers on the line weren't any better than the baggy pants he already had, so he left them alone. A small garden in the back yard produced several carrots for breakfast.

The city park was covered with large trucks and small booths with bright colors. A large man who was tan, bald and covered with tatoos was dropping hay by the forkfuls along a tether line to a string of beautiful white horses. A lady in tight pants walked to the high grass followed by six skinny little dogs. Like grease on a skillet, they barked and snapped and leaped around in a circle, fighting for the attention of their master. Somewhere a lion roared and a pulley squeaked, ropes stretched and monkeys chattered...the noise was infectious.

Addy was afflicted with the smell the morning sun was sifting from the scene. Manure, sweat, dust, excitement, strange people in strange clothes, and...popcorn. That was the best smell of all and the worst, because it awoke the snake of hunger curled in his belly. The bottom of a glass box was still littered with the remains of a night's work at vending. His mouth watered. Everyone seemed so busy, Addy was sure no one would miss the stale kernels, but the minute he reached his hand into the box, it was like the cogs to a great machine had been jammed.

"Hey, kid, get outta there. Charlotte, call the boss and tell him he's got another louse to haul into town." Muscles were bulging all around Addy as a man twirled him about. A large hand was locked on the shoulder of his stolen shirt. The shirt ripped at the armpits and his tightly rolled wardrobe spilled into the dust at his feet.

"Wait," said Addy, "I'll work for it. Don't call the police. I'm sorry." Addy's pleading was swallowed by the booming laugh of the strong man. Others gathered and joined in.

"Another runaway."

"Throw him to the lions."

"Let Elsa give him a big squeeze until his guts comes out his nose."

Frantic over what the crowd might do, Addy squirmed and dropped down to his knees. When he did, his arms went up and he slid free of the shirt, at the same time escaping the grasp of the strong man.

With the instinct of a wild animal, he spiraled around a tent wire and vaulted to the top of a wooden crate. The crowd cheered. In both fear and pleasure, Addy climbed higher, using the wires like tree vines to reach the main support of a power pole.

"All right, lads, you've had your fun," came a loud, but calm voice. The murmur below halted and Addy looked down. He found himself staring at the face of an old man whose wispy gray hairs barely covered a brown-speckled scalp.

"Come on down, son," said the man.

Addy clung to the power pole and stared at

the crowd, who stared at him. A man in a black coat and hat arrived.

"That's enough. You people get back to work," said the man. "I'm not paying you to play around with every little tramp that sneaks in here. Now clear out."

The bald man had to support his neck with one hand to look up at Addy. He smiled, then shook his head, "You done good, kid, to sally up there. Now get down before you break your neck."

Then it hit Addy why he had come in the first place.

"Wait," said Addy, switching hands to the tent wire and burning his palms as he slid down to the canvas and somersaulted off the edge of the tent. Pain shot through his ankles as he landed, but he kept it to himself and smiled.

"I've come to join the circus," said Addy, dropping to one knee in front of the man in the black coat and stretching out his arms for show.

The kind old man laughed and dropped down to one knee in front of his boss along with Addy, "Ah, give the kid a chance, Trooper."

The man in the black coat turned and scoffed, "Look kid, it takes a lot more than a few somersaults to join a circus. Go back to your folks. You don't know what you're getting into here." He removed his top hat long enough to wipe his face and forehead with a handkerchief. Another group of performers caught his attention and he groaned as he marched away to yell at the one setting a spike.

Addy looked hopefully into the face of the quiet man, but the man just pursed his lips and shook his head. The clothes from the orphanage had been trampled and Addy reached for his torn shirt and the pants with the rainbow suspenders.

24

"They don't look your size. They belong to your dad?"

"No," said Addy, "It's my clown costume."

"Oh," said the man. "You still hungry?"

"Yes," said Addy.

"Come on. I'll feed you. Then you'll have to go home."

Chapter Six

TILII

"So you want to be a clown," the man said, leading the way through an opening into a long narrow tent.

"I am a clown," said Addy. "It's in me."

"Well, we all have a little clown in us, I guess, but only a few have the heart that it takes to be a really good clown." Addy searched the face of the old man for understanding. When he caught his glance, there was a momentary glimmer of recognition, as if they had met before. Addy sensed a feeling of sadness behind the brown eyes, despite the smiling face. The flickering warmth faded and the man turned away.

"Is this where you live?" asked Addy.

The man stepped over a row of water buckets and chortled as he opened a trunk.

"Just in between shows, kid," came the muffled reply. The man rummaged around until he found a bag full of salami and cheese. The buckles on the lid clattered as it dropped into place. Addy read the worn gold letters on the front: T.I.L.II.

Accepting the bag of victuals, Addy nodded and backed away.

"Is that your name...Tilii?"

The old man laughed and sat down on his trunk.

"No, they're initials really, but that's what I go by in whiteface."

"Whiteface?" Addy asked, gnawing on the

26

salami.

"Whiteface is what we call the makeup we wear in the circus. See, I'm a clown and they call me Tilly." Addy's eyes brightened and he listened intently as the clown continued. "I didn't have much time to think of a name when I got the job. I was doing a night club act and hauling feed sacks during the day. Somebody offered me a chance to clown and they said 'What's your handle?' so I looks at my trunk and says 'Tilly.'"

The man's smile was contagious and Addy felt comfortable with him. Addy bit off a chunk of cheese and gazed down the row of trunks.

"This is clown alley," said Tilly. "We use the water pails for clean up and we each have a trunk and a crate. It's been home for about twenty years."

"What do you do for an act?"

"I do a bum in the depression routine, but I also have to ride bikes and horses, drive wagons, load trains, set up and break down, sell popcorn. Not only are clowns the best athletes in the circus, but you have to know all the acts because you work the riggings when you mimic the other performers. I've had to do trapeze, wire, crash land, drop into nets, balance without a net, and jump on and off horses. All for twenty-five dollars a week.

"Clowns also make their own costumes, practice on their own time, and...you gotta be able to think fast. Yeah, that's probably the most important thing about clowning."

"Can you get me a job?"

"Look, kid, I know things are tough out there, but working at a circus is no party."

Addy dropped the cheese into the bag and rolled it up tight. He straightened and stared at the clown with all the impatience his years of wanting and waiting had collected.

"Do you have a family?" Addy asked coldly.

"I had a wife once," Tilly's eyes darkened, "and a boy."

"Well, I don't have nobody. I'm an orphan, Tilly. I read a report that said I was abandoned at some park. Then the guy who runs the orphanage got a paper that says somethin' about foster care. For the last four years I've been pullin' plows for the buzzard while the snotty-nosed babies with cute faces gets picked by sweet-smellin' church people in fancy cars."

"I'm sorry..."

"No, don't be. I'm not sorry. I got nobody to tell me what to do. I'm decidin' what's what now and I want to be a clown." Addy gripped his bag of food, picked up his clothes, and wiped his mouth on his sleeve. "Thanks for the grub, Tilly."

"Wait."

"Yeah?"

"What's your handle?"

Addy smiled and raised one eyebrow as he looked over his shoulder at the clown from the half-open tent flap. He squeezed the roll of clothes with one hand and imagined himself dancing across the circus arena. A beautiful girl pirouetted in circles under his arm and his pants bobbed at the end of the rainbow suspenders.

"Baggy."

"Okay, Baggy, meet me back here in about an hour."

Addy saluted and left.

Chapter Seven

The Music Man

Murmurs were rising with the heat of the day as Addy walked along the midway, the main row of circus attractions. Animals yawned, a lion growled, and a chimpanzee screeched. The warm sun on the circus dust smelled sweet like the breath of the dairy cows in the winter. A boy with two buckets nearly ran into Addy and the water sloshed across their bare feet.

"Look out, tramp," said the boy, his dark eyes flashing at Addy. A cheek muscle in the boy's face bulged as he set his jaw; his sallow face and sunken eyes gave the impression that inside his skinny young frame was the mind of an old man. Sensing the anger, Addy quickly stepped to one side and tried in vain to appease the sour face with a smile.

The water carrier cleared his throat and spat, just missing Addy's big toe. Then he returned Addy's smile with a chuckle and continued on his way.

"Swine," Addy whispered under his breath.

The lyrical note of a small calliope danced across the yard on a puff of wind and Addy darted between the tents in search of its source. Skipping over stakes and ropes, Addy was lured to a tent with the flaps open where a small man with a long oiled mustache was turning a large music box. His four small monkeys were climbing a ladder and shooting down a small slide as he played the music on his portable organ. Whenever the music stopped, one monkey would squeal and take a seat on the bench by the music man. When only two of them were left on the slide and the music stopped, a terrible fight broke out until one monkey went screaming and flailing his arms to the lap of his master. The remaining monkey jumped to the top of the slide and the man played the notes of victory: dum-ta-ta-ta!

Addy clapped and the small man turned to thank his audience. Silver-blue eyes sparkled from a leathery face.

"Hello, lad. It's a bit early for spectators, isn't it."

"Yeah, I'm waitin' for Tilly."

"You a friend of his?"

"Well, sort of. He's helpin' me get a job."

"A job?" the man asked. "You're better off running along, lad. You don't want to join up with this circus."

"Why?"

"They're a tough lot on the likes of you. Oh, Tilly, he's a good 'un, but there's a bunch that'll razz you 'til you harden up like a cold dead rat in the sewer."

Barley's face floated in front of Addy as he listened. He could hear the old man thumping down the steps to the hall, yelling at the small bodies that scrambled just out of reach, "Get to work, you sewer rats, or I'll skin you and use your hides for seat covers." The gnarled hand landed on his shoulder and Addy tightened to receive the blow, but as he turned, his nightmare disappeared. He was looking into Tilly's smiling face.

"There you are, Baggy. I've been looking all over for you."

"I..." Addy faltered as he began an apology.

"The boss says he's sorry, but he can't hardly

pay the crew he has. Take this." Tilly handed Addy
two dollars. "Buy yourself some shoes and a pair of
pants. Maybe then you can hire on somewhere for a
really decent job."

The money wavered slightly in Addy's open
palm so Tilly closed Addy's fingers over the bills.
The boy searched Tilly's eyes and sensed a deepness
he had seen only once before – yesterday, when he
said goodbye to Skunker, only Skunker didn't know
it was goodbye.

Tilly's mouth drooped into his best frown and
the organ began to play a sad melody. The men
laughed and Addy realized he was staring. He
clasped his bundle with both hands and brushed
past Tilly without a word.

"Hey, we weren't laughing at you, kid," but
Addy didn't wait for the rest of the speech. He ran
off the circus grounds and across the field of a small
farm until he could bury himself in the sanctuary of
a haystack.

Chapter Eight

Robi

The cheese tasted sour and the meat felt greasy going down, but Addy ate it all and wiped his hands on the old hay. Two dollars was a reassuring sum for a boy on the run and he stuffed it into one of the stolen socks and put the socks in a pocket of the blazer. He checked the rest of his belongings and then used the pant legs to tie a knot around the package. It would be easier to carry that way.

It was too soon to show his face around town, but Addy figured he could blend in with the crowd at the circus. Maybe if he saw what the other performers were doing, he could plan a stunt that would impress Tilly's boss enough that he would hire him.

There was a charge at the gate and Addy had to duck down behind the park fence to untie his clothes to get to the money. From the sock, Addy pulled out the hidden bills then glanced down at his torn pants and soiled shirt. It might be safer to wear the blazer over the dirty clothes, Addy thought, so the police wouldn't spot his scruffy appearance. Or maybe Barley had alerted them about the coat. Addy decided Barley wasn't smart enough to miss the jacket and he put it on.

After his admittance through the gate, Addy used a quarter to buy a hot dog and a soda pop and put the remaining money back in the sock. There was still time to look around, but Addy avoided the tents of the performers and walked along a row of animal cages. It was a relief not to have to think about Skunker or Barley or dinner or the fields or anything to do with the orphanage. Addy was content to just be a boy at the circus. He wasn't even thinking about clowning when he heard a man yell and a tiger rocked one of the cages with a loud growl.

From behind the end of the cage Addy could see someone was prodding the tiger with a barbed rod.

"Get up, you lazy cat," shouted the hidden voice.

"Hey," Addy interrupted and he stepped behind the cage to stop the intruder, walking right into the wide rounded arms of the strong man who had grabbed him earlier in the day at the popcorn machine.

"So, the little tramp is here," the man teased. Addy choked as the man raised him off the ground by an iron lock on his clothes at the back of his neck. A piece of hot dog dropped out of Addy's mouth and the paper cup of pop bounced off his knee. The man let the rod fall and fingernails burned into Addy's shoulder as the man's free hand spun the boy around with a death grip on his collar bone.

"You want to see the kitty," the man sneered, his breath poisoning Addy as he spoke. "Here's my little kitty. She loves little boys." With that the man shoved Addy's face up to the bars of the cage and the tiger struck out with a paw, slicing the air only a foot from Addy's face.

"Ahh," Addy screamed and the sock full of money dropped at his feet.

The tiger narrowed its eyes and lifted puffy cheeks full of whiskers as it hissed and backed away from the commotion.

"Why looky here," said the man, "a bonus,"

and with his free hand, he whisked the sock full of change into a pocket.

"Robi, what are you doing?" came a voice from behind the cage. As the tiger crouched low along the floor of the cage, Addy froze, too afraid to speak, too afraid to close his eyes.

"I have Elsa's dinner, Tony. It's my little friend from this morning." With one hand still molded around the collar of Addy's coat, the man swung to face his friend, whipping Addy against the bars of the cage in the process.

"Lay off the kid, Robi. We have a show to do."

"Trooper said he wanted action tonight. How about we give the boss a new twist to the show."

The newcomer grabbed Addy's arm stretching him away from Robi. One of Addy's feet touched the ground giving him the chance to gulp a breath of air before the animal trainer pulled Addy back off the ground.

"I'm going to bring the boy out with me tonight. We'll put him in a cage in the ring and the cats will go crazy."

"You're drunk, Robi," said Tony grabbing Addy again and shoving the man only slightly away with his best punch.

Three horses stamped nervously on their line and the tiger continued to hiss and roar as the men fought. For a second Addy was free. For a second, his feet touched the ground, but Addy was powerless under Robi's grasp. Two hands took a fresh hold of the lapels of Addy's jacket and he was tossed through the air into the dancing legs of the tethered horses. The last thing Addy felt was the smack of a hoof whacking the side of his head. Blackness consumed him like the darkness at the bottom of the farm well.

Chapter Nine

Dawn

When Addy opened his eyes, he couldn't see. There was a heavy weight covering his body and a stifling smell surrounded his face. His head throbbed when he tried to move his neck and none of his limbs seemed to work. Flecks of dirt crept into his mouth when he tried to lick his lips and straw poked at his eyes. He wiggled his toes and dug his fingers into the warm earth. Then he recognized it...the smell, the wetness, the grainy matter riddled with hay...it was manure.

With his head to one side, he struggled to move one sore arm. His hand pushed away the dirt in front of his face. He worked, in darkness, in confusion. When the light filtered through to his face, Addy tried to bring his legs up to his chest. The pain echoed in his ears with a loud drumming as he freed his body from the pile of manure and straw.

When Addy could sit, he spit out the manure he had licked into his mouth and tried to brush the annoying bits of hay away from his eyes. He felt the blood caked on the side of his head and reached nervously for the wound above his ear. There was only a small dig into his scalp, but the kick had split his ear and left a small lump on his head.

Sickness nagged at his stomach and it was some minutes before Addy could remember what had happened. He braced his back against the short cement wall that bordered the pile of manure and looked about the grounds. This was the city park in Copperstock. It was a mess. There were papers

35

flitting about and popcorn kernels everywhere. It was dawn. The sun was barely up over the trees surrounding the country town.

This was where the circus was.

Where was the circus? Addy stopped thinking momentarily when something tried to rise up from his stomach. He took a deep breath and looked at his legs. Soda pop had spilled on his pants and he was wearing his ripped shirt and the blazer. The socks!

Addy searched his pockets. The drumming in his head increased while he pulled himself up to his knees. The blazer pocket was empty, the socks were gone. He tried the pockets of his pants. The knife was gone. The matches were gone. And the change was gone. With outstretched hands, Addy rummaged through the wet straw. He found one sock and turned it inside out. It was empty.

In a line of trash cans overflowing with cartons, bags and circus flyers, Addy searched for the rest of his possessions. With an effort to keep his head at a level position, Addy dug into the garbage. The bright suspenders were easy to find and when he pulled, the baggy pants sprung loose from the barrel along with soggy popcorn bags and wadded up napkins. He shook them out once and rolled them into a ball, before sitting back down on the cement.

The wound still throbbing in his head, Addy tried to replay yesterday over in his mind. The circus was here. I came to the circus. I paid to get in. I went to see the animals. Addy winced as the memory of Robi's face seared up in front of him. The man grabbed me. He put me up against the bars of the cage. Then...Addy swooned for a moment.

Addy touched his wound gently and continued probing the dark path of the memory. A man came

36

and tried to stop him and they fought and I fell against the horses. The kick reverberated in the stillness of the dawn as if he could still hear it and a tear rolled down Addy's cheek, leaving a dirty path as it dropped onto his chest. Realizing Robi must have taken his money and buried him in the manure pile, Addy faced the truth. He was alone. He had no money.

The sputtering of an old truck caught Addy's attention and he watched the truck pull into the park some distance away. A short man yanked a rake from the bed of the truck and used it to sweep up the garbage along the road. There was no place to go, but Addy knew he would have to move away from Copperstock to be free of Barley and life at the orphanage.

Chapter Ten

Fever

Hunger and depression stalked Addy like desperate wild animals. For days Addy stumbled through the rocky New England woods, drinking at streams, falling exhausted into a sweaty dirty heap at the end of the day. Haunting eyes watched from the darkness at night. Forest voices whispered through the trees. Addy listened, but he understood nothing. He looked over his shoulder. He watched his feet as he walked up each hill and down into the briars of each muggy vale.

On the third day, he was no longer concerned with his capture and he was no longer depressed. Only hunger remained. Then came the town of Fever. Curled into a ball on a soft bank at the side of a dirt road, Addy closed his eyes and let the sun rise over his cold tired body. He ran a finger along the seams of his blazer and pulled at threads here and there for something to chew on.

When one finger slipped inside an opening in the satin lining, Addy sat up quickly and jerked the blazer open. A hidden pocket! Inside the small breast pocket was a folded dollar bill. Juices burned in the pit of his stomach when Addy thought about the food he could buy with a dollar.

Ordinarily the sound of a car would have caused Addy to flee into hiding, but the dollar had raised his hopes and he stood quickly to catch a ride into town. Addy was so weak that the effort was more than his body could take. He reeled and collapsed back onto the grass.

"Say, lad, can I give you a lift into town?" asked a voice.

The dizziness cleared momentarily as Addy peered into the face of a man in a black suit who was bending over him.

"Are you all right?"

"Yeah, I'm fine," said Addy, using an extended arm for assistance as he hobbled shakily to the car.

Once seated, Addy leaned back against the door and smiled meekly at the man. The smell of cookies exploded with aroma when the man opened a tin and allowed Addy to help himself.

"Slow down there, pal," said the man as Addy chased one cookie after another down into the empty aching pit of his stomach.

"You kids," the driver continued. "You think you can take on the world on a whim. You always think your ma and pa are wrong, so you take off on your own and what happens? You end up hungry and somebody else's ma or pa has to take care of you."

The lecture may not have ended there, but Addy was too busy feeding himself to listen. It took concentration to find enough saliva to moisten the dry cookies to make room for more and to keep from choking as he stuffed them down.

"Where are you going?" the man asked.

Quickly, Addy disguised his fear with an answer.

"To the feed store." It was a make-believe answer to sway the opinion of the man. He did not want to appear homeless.

"Oh, really. You friends of the Salendorfs?"

"No." Pretending to choke a little, Addy tried

39

to think.

"Easy does it. I think you ought to see the doc. You look like you're in pretty rough shape."

"No, I'm fine. I'm meetin' someone at the feed store." Addy stopped for a second and wiped his face on his arm. "Uncle Peter lent me plenty of money for the trip, but a hobo took my wallet at the circus in Copperstock. Now I have to meet Uncle Peter's cousin to borrow some more money."

This was a wonderful story, Addy thought to himself. He didn't know lying could be so much fun.

"Where are you going?"

"After my ma and pa passed away, my Aunt Gertie wrote me from Columbus..."

"Columbus?"

"It's a little town about two days north of here."

"Hmm. Never heard of it."

"I got a job there workin' for my cousin Jack."

"Well, here ya be. This is the feed store."

The car popped and slid to a halt in front of a large red barn with its garage door propped open with a four-by-four. Regretfully, Addy popped the lid back into place over the cookies and waved goodbye as the Ford rattled on down the road. Addy took two steps, slowly, waiting for the car to turn and disappear as it headed into the thick of Fever, a town of two-story wooden-framed buildings and very few people.

"Can I help you?" asked a man in a leather apron. His black mustache twitched as he leaned against the frame of the door and folded his arms across his chest, eyeing Addy suspiciously.

"Could you point the way to the grocery?"

"One block up and two blocks to the left." Wiping the ends of his mustache with his gritty hand, the man looked the boy up and down.

It was time to disappear and Addy waved his thanks as he walked weakly away. The pain in his stomach pinched uncomfortably at each step. Not having ever gorged himself on cookies before, Addy wasn't sure how long the pain would last.

A horse trough with some scummy-looking water sufficed for a quick wash and a drink. Addy used his baggy pants as a towel and then pulled on the soiled blazer to cover his tattered shirt. Hopefully, he was clean enough to avoid being arrested or thrown out of town as a tramp.

The knot in Addy's stomach tightened and he dropped down behind some trash cans to throw up into the dirt. He was so hungry he wanted to pick up the half-digested cookies in his hands, but the need for an outhouse stopped him and he weaved his way to the back of a store where he found an old privy.

Addy had to return to the trough for a second bath before he could think about food again. A handful of ice from a soda vending machine helped to quiet the twisting of his gut. After resting on some steps and sucking on the ice, Addy began to feel better. He rummaged through some garbage and found half of a hot dog. He chewed it slower this time and was grateful when his stomach accepted it.

With his dollar, Addy purchased some strings of beef jerky, a chocolate bar and a hard roll of bread. From a large wooden tray outside the grocery store, Addy lifted an apple and an orange and continued on to the next block.

Surrounding a statue in the village green of a central park, a circle of small children giggled and shared their whimsical dramas of make believe. Addy was drawn to their laughter like a ship to a beacon, coming home. He sat on a curb by the park and watched as he ate.

One boy with a pug nose and freckles looked up from where he lay wrestling a younger opponent. Skunker's face appeared momentarily, drawing Addy back to Wood's Home.

"Addy?" He could hear Skunker. He could see the deep brown eyes staring up at him, hoping for reassurance. "Addy, you won't ever leave, will you?"

The children's silence startled Addy away from his dream, from his lonely world.

"Who are you?" asked the little boy.

"I'm a clown."

"Where did you come from," the child asked timidly.

"Somebody made a wish...and here I am," said Addy, resorting to his childish grin. Addy still felt weak and light-headed, but it didn't stop him from making faces and swirling around in front of the children. He swooped over to the statue to grab a child's ball. The blazer flapped at his side as Addy hopped about to face the frightened child. Addy juggled the apple, the orange and the ball in perfect unison and the children smiled.

"Wow, a clown." The children sat and clapped in admiration as Addy continued juggling, balancing on one foot and then hopping up to the ledge of the statue to juggle some more. The ball landed in the lap of the little boy, the orange in a hand behind Addy's back, and the apple dropped to Addy's mouth where he clenched it in his teeth and chomped it sloppily, like an old horse.

The children's laughter was encouraging and Addy bowed. When they screamed for more, Addy dropped to all fours and drooled and growled like a mad dog as he circled his audience, still eating his precious apple. A small girl in a red-checkered dress and a white pinafore squealed in delight and Addy cartwheeled for her and stood on his hands.

When the children stopped clapping, Addy righted himself and found that he had been discovered by three lads about his own size.

"Hey, freak, what are you doing here?" asked one.

"Get away from my sister," said another.

The act was too good to spoil so Addy grabbed a cap off the shortest of the three and leaped up to the statue, striding the back of the iron horse with the poise of a general. Then he felt faint and tried to hide it by grabbing the horse's neck.

The boys were looking for a fight and Addy's antics did not amuse them. They threw handfuls of gravel and sand at Addy until someone yelled at them to stop.

"Hey you guys."

They turned and faced a girl in a blue cotton dress. She was about their size, but she held her ground with a firm stance, her hands clenched over her hips, her knees locked, her long brown braids thrown defiantly to the back.

"Oooo, we're scared." One of the boys teased the girl and began to circle her cautiously. "It's the old widow's little orphan girl."

Addy's face brightened. He jumped silently off the horse and headed for the others.

"Cut it out, Marcus," the girl said, fixed in a deadly stare of eye warfare with the boy.

"Go eat dirt, Raisin."

"Why don't you pick on someone your own size, Marcus, like Zeb's dog."

Marcus puffed up in anger and stepped close to the girl's face. Addy jumped between them, but as

43

he did, the children scattered.

"Ditch it," one of the smaller boys said, "Old Man Larsen's comin'."

The smaller children scattered. The three boys gave Addy and Raisin a warning shove and walked away.

Raisin looked at Addy and shook her head. It was a look of sympathy, but Addy felt suddenly ashamed.

"You kids stop playing on that statue." The man who had reached the edge of the park was now shaking a finger in Addy's face and yelling. "I've told you kids to quit hangin' around the park like a bunch of hobos. You stay off...hey," he said, interrupting himself as he thrust his bristly gray mustache up to Addy for a closer look. Old Man Larsen lowered his glasses and licked his cracked lips. "You're not from around here. I think you'd better come with me."

Addy straightened and smiled confidently. He would simply repeat the story he had used at the feed store.

"I'm meetin' someone. You see, my Aunt Gertie from Columbus..."

"Where?"

"Columbus. She sent for me and Uncle Peter's cousin's gonna meet me to get me the money I need to get to Columbus."

"Peter, ya say. Peter who?"

"No, it's his cousin."

"What's his cousin's name?" the old man asked.

Addy drew a blank for a moment, just enough time for Raisin to cut in.

"We were just leaving, Mr. Larsen," said Raisin.

44

"Oh, I see. He's with you, is he? Well, you should know better than to be stirrin' up trouble in the park, Raisin. With all your poor Aunt Adelaide has to contend with. Now you get yourselves outta here and get back home."

"Yes, sir, Mr. Larsen." Raisin tugged at Addy's sleeve. Addy was in a bit of a trance of disbelief over why Raisin would have defended him, but he grabbed his tied-up-bundle of clothes and gratefully followed Raisin, dipping his head respectfully to the gnarled old man.

The man cleared his throat and turned, still grumbling as he left, his oversized suit wrinkling as he walked away.

Chapter Eleven

Anabelle Lee

In silence, Addy followed Raisin to a wide dirt road that headed north out of town. The heat of the day was building early and what few maple trees there were along the road, were wilting in the dust and heat.

"Thanks," said Addy when the girl stopped to face him.

"You drifters are all alike," she snapped. Startled by the girl's abrupt change, Addy stepped back and watched cautiously as the girl continued to scold him. She was shorter than Addy, but she stood with her knees locked back and her hands planted firmly at the hips, as she had at the park. Raisin reminded Addy of his last school teacher, who had found many opportunities for such lectures.

"Things get a little tough in one place, and just like a cow, you think the grass is better along the road, so you break through the fence. Then somebody else has to take care of you or take you home. Don't you ever get tired of hoppin' fences? What are you doin' trampin' around Connecticut anyway?"

The small upturned nose and long brown eyelashes were just too cute to be intimidating. Addy smiled, but it only angered her more and the girl took a deep breath to appear more ferocious.

"Who do you think you are, coming in here like the Pied Piper? You almost got arrested."

Two long brown braids shook their propeller-like ribbons as the young peacemaker tried her best to point Addy to the road of righteousness.

"You certainly don't think *you'll* ever be in a circus? Why, just look at you."

Addy looked at his dirty wrinkled trousers and blazer. He felt the sticky sweat where the jacket rubbed his bare skin through the torn shirt. For a moment he remembered lying in bed at the home, exhausted from the work in the fields, too tired to wash, just hot and sweaty and falling asleep...until Barley's hand at his throat would bring him back to reality...and back to the field.

"I guess I look pretty dirty," Addy said.

Suddenly ashamed at her boldness, Raisin recoiled and asked apologetically if Addy was hungry.

"I just ate breakfast."

"Oh, well, I better go," said Raisin.

Addy watched her turn and then blurted out, "Are you an orphan?" When Raisin looked back, Addy could feel his cheeks turning red and he looked down at his bare feet.

"Not really," said Raisin, "I live with my Aunt Adelaide, except she's not really my aunt. She was a friend of my mother's. My father kind of wandered off..."

It was Raisin's turn to be embarrassed, so Addy cut in.

"Yeah, I know how it goes. I guess my old lady dumped me in a park when I was a baby and my old man musta been too broke to take care of me. I saw some papers about it, but it didn't make much sense to me. What about your ma?"

"She died, some years back." Addy decided Raisin was pretty when she wasn't angry. He could see why she had to be so tough. Sometimes it was hard to be a kid.

"Is your aunt good to ya?"

"Yeah, she's swell. She's the smartest person in Fever."

"Where?"

"Here. This is Fever."

"Oh."

"But you won't find work here. You should go north to Glendale," Raisin said pointing up the naked dusty dirt road that disappeared into fields of corn. "There's work there," she said hesitating, "for an honest person." Then she brushed the dust off the apron of her blue dress and flounced the puffy sleeves. With a toss of her plaited hair, she spun on one heel and bid Addy goodbye.

"You're right," said Addy. The girl stopped and looked over her shoulder as Addy squirmed and nervously tightened his roll of clothes against one hip, avoiding Raisin's glare.

"I ain't much to look at and I am sort of a mess," Addy said, Then he straightened. "But someday I'm gonna be a clown in a circus."

The girl pursed her lips and shook her head. When she continued to walk away, Addy took a step forward and raised his voice.

"I'm not askin' for favors. I can take care of myself."

"Oh, really? What would you have done in jail?"

"I said I was grateful for the help, but how do ya think I made it this far? Nobody gives me breakfast in the morning or clothes to wear, or shoes," Addy said. They both looked self-consciously at the brown leather shoes on the girl's feet. "And as far as breakin' fences, I..."

When Addy raised his voice, the girl shushed

48

him and looked around, "Shh, keep your voice down. I shouldn't even be talking to you."

Addy continued as if she hadn't interrupted. "I been pullin' a plow at an orphanage and the guy runnin' the place is a lousy bum. There weren't no green grass on our side of the fence. Mostly moldy bread, a stinkin' outhouse, and the back of a hand for thanks after a day's work. Nobody's never takin' me home. I either had ta bust out or stay there and rot."

Addy imagined his trunk parked in clown alley with the name BAGGY printed across the front. "My home hasn't happened yet, but it will, and I don't need no two-bit kid in pigtails to tell me what's right." Addy wiped the dead grass and dirt off his pants from where he had been rolling in the park.

"Fine," said the girl with a small pout of her lower lip.

Addy watched her step up to the wooden sidewalk in front of a cute house with flower pots in the windows.

"What's your handle?" Addy asked.

"My what?" said the girl.

"Your name."

"Oh." The girl thought and said, a little bit dreamily, "Anabelle Lee. And if you are a clown, then I am a bareback rider with six fine white horses that obey my every command."

Girls were the most confusing people Addy had ever met. As he watched her twirl around a post and brush her braids to her back, he tried to imagine her in sparkling leotards. Addy could hear the music introducing her act as she sprang into the ring.

"Really?" Addy teased, at a loss for words. The sharp tongue of the young lady had been replaced with the quiet imaginings of a circus soul, someone Addy could understand. Someone who shared his dreams. She had captured his fascination, but baffled his understanding. For once, Addy did not know what to say, nor did his feet lift him to the nearest railing to perform or free him from the embarrassing position he took of standing and watching his feet.

An innocent smile and cove-blue eyes tempted Addy to step in for a closer look until the mood was shattered with the high-pitched screech of an old woman, "RAI-SIN."

"Aunt Adelaide?" Addy asked.

"I better go," Raisin said, trotting briskly away. Addy turned and faced the empty-looking road to Glendale.

"Hey," Raisin yelled from down the block, "What's your name?"

"Addy."

"Goodbye, Addy."

From around the corner, an elderly woman in a straw hat and colorless clothes draped a loving arm about Raisin's shoulders. She cast a worried glance toward Addy and then escorted Raisin out of sight.

Chapter Twelve

Adelaide

Another road.

Addy sighed.

When thirst overcame him, he perched on a split-rail fence and fingered the young stalks of corn. The kernels were white and hard, but Addy picked the ripest one he could find and sat down on the ground to make a meal out of it. To the south, the tops of the houses in Fever were obscured by a grove of trees. To the north, there was no sight of Glendale. Empty pockets, hunger raw as snake bite, and sadness deeper than the eyes of a wounded dog were Addy's companions now.

There were no tears, just concentration. How long before someone would catch him stealing, Addy wondered. What would Barley do to him if the police returned him to Wood's Home? Ripping a small stalk up by the roots to appease the pain in his gut, Addy continued his thoughts. He peeled another ear of corn and lay back to chew it up and down as he searched the rolling clouds for an answer. A puffy-cheeked minstrel tooted a flute while a legless dog with a wispy tail followed close behind. The clouds comforted the lonely boy with their parade. If I don't find another circus, I'll die, said Addy to the flying minstrel.

Tired and hungry as he was, Addy had stopped paying attention to the sounds around him. A black car was only fifty feet away before he thought to drop into the corn. The car screeched to a halt.

"Shoot," Addy said, sure of his fate. Peeking through the stalks of corn, Addy watched a pair of black leather shoes with tiny pointed toes and high wide heels walk gracefully across the sand to his sanctuary. The figure belonging to the shoes said nothing. Addy wondered if he was hidden from view. Then he listened as the window of the car opened and a familiar voice called to him.

"Addy? It's okay. Me and my Aunt Adelaide came to get you."

It was a shy and thankful boy who rose to accept the offer. His eyes still fixed on the black pumps, Addy worked his way up to survey every detail: the slender legs in silk stockings; the gray skirt; the creamy ivory shirt; the tan wrinkled hands that showed under folded arms; the black and white brooch clasped tightly between the edges of a scalloped-lace collar; the tired, but gentle face with thin dry lips and heavy eye lids seemingly void of lashes; the sweep of the gray hair with some strands falling softly out from their assigned pins; and the smell of something sweet, like flowers.

Unable to contain herself, Raisin had pranced to Addy's side. "This is my Aunt Adelaide."

"Hello, Addy," said the woman, extending an arm. Addy wiped his hand on his coat and shook her hand. She had a strong grip for an old woman.

The boy looked shyly away and turned to fetch his pants and suspenders, still cached neatly in the corn.

"I'll bet you're hungry, Addy," said the girl, waiting restlessly for Addy to join her. Raisin seemed excited as she led Addy around to her door and guided him to the center of the front seat.

Raisin was altogether different from the

52

commandeering general who had broken up the brawl at the park and sent Addy packing to Glendale. Girls are definitely more complicated than boys, thought Addy, as he listened to Raisin explain her "plan."

"Addy, Aunt Adelaide says you can stay with us for awhile. She'll help you find a job. You probably won't be able to find a job in Fever, but Auntie says we can take you to Glendale and help you look. Besides, we need some help at our house. Right, Auntie?" Adelaide shook her head "yes" to reply and smiled at Addy as she put the car into gear and turned it around.

"Do you know how to put on shingles?" Raisin asked. Addy was still too flustered about his rescue to respond.

"All right, Raisin, that's enough. Give the boy a chance to speak." The woman glanced over at Addy while she was driving. It was an honest look and Addy felt humbled just by returning the gaze.

"I haven't got a lot to offer, son," she said, "but you are welcome to some good cooking in exchange for a few chores. We won't stand in the way of your plans. Raisin tells me you have your mind made up to be a clown."

"Yes, ma'am," said Addy.

"Addy, one more thing."

"Yes. ma'am," Addy repeated.

"You are to be a gentleman in my house. Do you know what that means?"

Addy smiled and looked at Raisin. "Yes, ma'am. I'm real good at bein' a gentleman."

Except for an occasional growl from Addy's stomach, the car was quiet after that. Bouncing along the dusty road, Addy thought about the little town of Fever. There would be no reason for Barley

53

to pass through such a small town and if he had a family to stay with, surely the police wouldn't bother him. The new hopes felt warm and comforting, casting the boy into sleep, to dream.

Chapter Thirteen

The Contest

In only a week, Addy had cleaned the entire barn and fixed all of the farm's failing fences. In return, Adelaide purchased clothes, shoes and gloves for Addy. Together they planned repairs for the rest of the outbuildings.

"Addy, Aunt Adelaide wants to know if she can put your baggy britches in the wash?"

From atop the roof of the hen house, Addy removed two nails he had clenched in his teeth and set the hammer to one side while he yelled back to Raisin, "Yep. Although, I ain't worn 'em yet."

"What are ya packing them around for then?"

"It's my clown costume."

"Oh." Raisin turned and ran back to the house, letting the screen door slam behind her. In seconds it banged again as she flew back out to the hen house with a sandwich.

"Auntie says she doesn't want lice getting into the house, but she told me not to tell you she said so. So don't say I did." With one hand coiled tightly around each rung of the ladder and the sandwich clenched in her teeth, Raisin cautiously pulled herself up to the top of the house where Addy was sprawled out along the peak of the roof to patch new shingles across the seam.

"How old are you, Raisin?"

"Almost eleven. How 'bout you?"

"Twelve," said Addy, breaking long enough to devour the thick bread and slices of canned lunchmeat.

"Really? I'll be twelve in a year."

Addy chuckled just before he set four more nails in his mouth to free up his hands for nailing. With ease he whacked each nail into place with only one blow.

"Did Barley teach you how to shingle a roof?"

"I don't know, Raisin. I think I was born knowin' how to do all this stuff because I don't remember Barley teachin' me anything."

"Did you go to school?"

"Yeah, for awhile."

"How long?"

With a look that sent the message to Raisin that she had asked her daily allowance of questions, Addy answered coldly, "Long enough."

For at least two minutes, Raisin sat on the ladder and watched Addy without interrupting. The silence made Addy wonder if he had hurt her feelings, so he asked her to bring up some more shingles – whatever she could carry.

"Addy, there's gonna be a talent show at our school? Do you want to go and watch? Maybe you'll want to do something in the talent show."

"What's a talent show?"

"Whoops," said Raisin, letting several shingles scatter the chickens below while she clung tighter to the ladder with one free hand.

"You all right?" mumbled Addy, through the nails in his mouth.

"Never mind," she said, "I was just climbing too fast. Anyway, a talent show is a contest where you do something in front of an audience, like sing or dance, and you get prizes."

"I don't know how ta sing or dance."

"If you're going to be a good clown, you're

going to have to do something. What are you going to do for your act?"

"Well, I been thinkin' 'bout that. I have some ideas. What are the prizes?" With increased interest, Addy had paused from nailing. Raisin had his full attention and she seemed pleased.

"First place gets five dollars and then there are a bunch of other things like a book, candy, and stuff."

"I dunno, Raisin."

"You weren't so shy in the park. I saw you juggling and jumping around. You can't just mope around here the rest of the summer."

"Look Raisin, people don't like me. They don't trust me. The people in town just think I'm passin' through and I'm nothin' but..."

"But what?"

Addy did not answer. He took a nail from his pocket and whacked it as hard as he could.

"Owwww," Addy yelled, wounding his thumb, causing the hammer to slide down into the pen, sending chickens squawking in a spasm of rustled feathers and beating wings.

"Ah, shhhoot," said Addy.

"Addy, shush." Raisin flashed a glance at the house and then scaled down the ladder to fetch the hammer.

While Addy sucked on his swollen thumb, Raisin took one more shot at her friend. "You're good, Addy, but you're not perfect. If you want to be perfect, you're going to have to work hard at it."

"Don't tell me 'bout workin' hard..."

From the center of the pen, Raisin interrupted and continued scolding her friend.

"I don't mean pulling a plow and stop telling me about your lousy life every time I try to talk to you. I mean about being a clown."

"I don't see you balancin' on any horses...Anabelle Lee," Addy teased. Flames of anger burned red in Raisin's cheeks. Her brown lashes flashed her discontent and she kicked the birds away in disgust.

"Raisin?" Addy yelled, but the girl propped the hammer on the bottom rung of the ladder and strutted defiantly back to the house. One more time, the screen door banged into its worn path.

Chapter Fourteen

The Orchard

When the call came for supper, Addy found himself staring at the ground from the loft of the barn. For hours he had been working out a stunt to use for the talent show. It couldn't hurt to try, he thought. Raisin was right. He needed to be ready to be a clown. Some day he would be the best clown ever, he thought as he ran in for supper.

"Addy, have you seen Raisin?" Aunt Adelaide asked.

"No, ma'am. At least not since the hen house."

"I've looked everywhere for her. Well, you go ahead and eat. I'll have a look around the farm again."

Still standing, Addy pushed in his chair and motioned for the woman to sit down.

"I'll look," he said.

Before Adelaide could argue, a scream sent them both running out the door.

"Raisin? Where are you?" yelled Adelaide from the porch.

Rosey, the old carriage horse, came trotting up from the creek bed, her reins dragging along the ground as she sashayed sideways into the garden.

"Whoa, Rosey," Addy said, grabbing the reins only seconds after Rosey had plowed through the tomatoes.

"Raisin?" Adelaide yelled again. There was no answer. Addy tied the mare to the porch railing.

When there was no response to Adelaide's frightened
call, Addy led the way down across the dry rocky
creek and up the other side to a lush meadow. The
pair stopped and listened. Still there was no answer
to Adelaide's worried cry.

The grass in the meadow was flattened in
areas where deer had slept, but there was no sign of
a little girl. Beginning to fear he had tempted his
bold friend to try something she wasn't ready for,
Addy searched the ground for hoofprints that might
indicate the direction the horse had fled.

"Adelaide," said Addy shyly, "It might be my
fault."

"Why?" said Adelaide, shading her eyes from
the sun as she scanned the field.

"Well, I kinda told Raisin she was fulla hot air
'bout ridin' horses in the circus."

"Oh, Addy," Adelaide began, unable to
continue. When Addy turned to look at the woman,
he saw her face was white and she seemed suddenly
faint.

"What is it?"

"Raisin's mother."

"What?"

"She wanted to be a trick rider..."

"Was she killed riding?" Addy asked, sensing
the unspoken sadness of death in her speech.

Adelaide nodded, "Yes."

"I'm sorry. I didn't know. I didn't mean to..."

"Please, Addy, find her. She's got to be all
right. She's all I have."

In the field Addy picked up a trail where the
dried grass had parted. He ran through the briars
and shrubbery, yelling for Raisin. Behind him, he
could hear Aunt Adelaide weeping. At the end of the
field, Addy found a trail that swung back through a

small grove of trees toward the house. He was almost to the barn when he heard a groan and called out again for Raisin.

Just then, where a spring had swamped the grass, Addy noticed the tracks of the mare.

"This way," he shouted to Adelaide and he followed the path Rosey had cut through the moist grass.

"Ohhhh," came the groan again, from the shade. A thick oak, whose arms spread out into the sunshine of the meadow like tentacles of a great beast, now hovered over Raisin like a predator.

"Here," said Addy, arriving first to Raisin's side. Raisin moaned and looked away. It wasn't until Adelaide stooped next to the girl that tears escaped over Raisin's dirt-stained cheeks.

"Oh child, what were you tying to do?" Adelaide asked as she checked Raisin over for injuries.

With a shy glance at Addy, Raisin said, "I was teaching Rosey to be a circus horse, but I forgot about the tree. I kinda crashed into it."

Convinced there were no serious injuries, Adelaide brushed the girl's bangs to one side to scold Raisin, "You scared me half to death, child," said Adelaide. "She's all right, Addy. Maybe you could fetch the wheelbarrow for me."

"It's okay, ma'am, I'll get her." Addy gently raised Raisin off her pile of sticks and despite her groans, he smiled.

"I'm gonna call the doc anyway, just to make sure," said Adelaide, running on ahead. "And I've got just the remedy," she laughed, "guaranteed to cure the ailments of all bossy bareback riders."

"Uh oh," said Raisin, imagining the foul-tasting liquid Aunt Adelaide would have waiting for her when she was put to bed.

Addy crossed the creek bed, struggling to balance Raisin's weight over the rocks. He watched as another tear rolled down Raisin's cheek and she closed her eyes.

"Guess you're not perfect yet...Anabelle."

Raisin shook her head "no" and winced in pain.

Addy felt strong carrying Raisin, although it wasn't easy. He took a deep breath and set his teeth together under the strain. It had felt right to run through the briars, to stop Adelaide from crying, to find Raisin alive, and to carry her home. It was a feeling Addy loved, walking home, even if it was Raisin's home.

"Let's not be fightin' each other, okay?" Addy asked.

"Okay," said Raisin, "just don't drop me."

Chapter Fifteen

The Barn

It took a month for Addy to work hard enough to pay off the clothes, including the shoes, and to finally receive a dollar, his first wages. He worked harder for Adelaide than he had ever worked at the orphanage. He worked out of love, not fear. Although he missed Skunker, and wondered if perhaps he had been adopted by now, the memory of Barley's rotten breath and hard cold hands were buried away in a deep unused corner of Addy's mind.

Adelaide's list of chores was endless, but Addy had to admit, the farm was certainly shaping up.

"The chickens are out again. I guess I'd better fix the fence around the pen," said Addy.

"I'll get eggs," said Raisin and she grabbed a basket as she followed Addy out the door. After Addy's work on the fence, they hunted through the barn for any eggs the escaped chickens might have laid.

"I guess I'm not very good at bareback riding," Raisin said.

"Oh, you just need a little practice," said Addy.

"Thanks." Raisin smiled.

"'Bout twenty years is all."

"You rat," Raisin said, pushing Addy into the straw.

"Don't call me that."

"Why not?" laughed Raisin, tossing a pitchfork of straw over Addy when he tried to surface.

Brandishing handfuls of straw, Addy retaliated, drowning his opponent in the process.

"Because I'll kill ya," Addy laughed, burying Raisin under more of the dusty yellow blanket.

"Addy, I can't breathe."

With one brush of his arm, Addy magically uncovered a path across Raisin's face. He blew away the chaff on her face and they giggled.

"Get off of me, you lug," Raisin said.

"Catch me," Addy teased. He scaled up the ladder to the loft.

With a war whoop of pure delight, Addy leapt over the bales of hay. Boards creaked as he swung from a cross beam. When he noticed Raisin was silent, Addy dropped to his belly on the floor of the loft and peeked over the edge at Raisin. He peered into the mysterious face of the girl, who was still lying at the foot of the ladder. She seemed fascinated by Addy's game, content to just watch and listen.

"Girls are strange," said Addy.

"Boys are dumb," said Raisin.

"Raisin?" Addy asked, because he did not know what else to say. But Raisin did not have time to answer.

The heavy barn door slid across its track, sending the soft summer light of dusk rippling through the dusty air of the barn.

"Raisin? Addy?" Aunt Adelaide studied the faces of the children as they stared at one another and at her. "Bring me those eggs so I can fix your dinner." She smiled one of her special lovely smiles, adding, "stop messin' up my pile of straw."

"Yes, ma'am," said Addy, scaling back down the ladder.

After the screen door was heard banging into place, Addy asked, "Why does she call you Raisin?"

Combing the straw from her hair with her fingers, Raisin told a short story. It was a relief to Addy to have something to talk about.

"Auntie says I was born early on account of my daddy had been drinkin' and he pushed Mama around a bit until she got mad and raised a pistol at him to scare him off. When my daddy hit her, the gun went off and hit Mama in the leg. The shock musta started the delivery because I came along about four hours later. Auntie thinks my daddy ran off because he was afraid he'd killed my mama and they would've put him in jail. He's one of those people who get real crazy in closed places."

Addy nodded his head as he listened. They walked slowly to the house.

"I guess bein' as how I was early, I was little," said Raisin, looking up at Addy. "Well, Mama went away for awhile, but the last thing she said to Auntie was 'Take care of her Adelaide, she's nothin' but a little red raisin.'"

Addy held the door open for Raisin, who was cradling a full basket of eggs. Then he smiled apologetically at Adelaide when he let the screen door slam behind him.

Chapter Sixteen

The Stream

"Eat your peas, Raisin," said Aunt Adelaide, cutting her pork neatly into squares.

"Raisin, you asked me one time if there wasn't anything I couldn't do," said Addy.

"Yeah?" asked Raisin.

"Say yes, Raisin, not yeah," instructed Auntie.

"Yes?" repeated Raisin, trying to flaunt a proper British accent.

Addy swallowed a mouthful and continued. "Well, there is one thing. I don't read too great and I want ya to look somethin' up in the library for me."

"Good for you, Addison," said Adelaide. "I'm glad to hear you are using your mind. I knew you had it in you."

"Well, truth is, ma'am, I wanted Raisin to look up somethin' for me 'bout clownin'. I'm plannin' an act for the talent show."

Adelaide waggled her head in protest and Raisin smiled in delight.

"Of course I will, Addy," said Raisin.

"One more thing," said Addy.

Raisin looked up from her plate, "Yes?"

"I left some papers somewheres 'cause I didn't understand any of it. I guess I didn't really wanna understand it, but I do now."

"Okay," said Raisin.

Addy looked at Adelaide and asked, "Could you drive us there?" Adelaide looked back at Addy and smiled. Because of her good cooking and endless chores, Addy had put on weight and muscle over the summer. His broad tan shoulders straightened under her stare; his eyes met hers and pleaded, as if in prayer. It was more than the file. What Addy really wanted was an answer to his past. What had happened to his parents? Looking into the gray gentle eyes of Adelaide made Addy wish he could bury his hopes and dreams and stay here...forever.

"Of course, my dear," said Adelaide and they finished their supper in silence, in thought.

* * *

It wouldn't be hard to find the two big boulders where he had pinned the file folder down under rocks, thought Addy, as the old Ford bumped along. Adelaide commented on the country and told Raisin many stories as they drove past the fields and woods that had marked Addy's flight into Fever. His first few days of freedom haunted him as they neared the stream: the expectations, the running, the circus, the hunger, the defeat, and now he had returned to this spot. Perhaps now, after nights of hearing the word "abandoned" over and over again in his mind, after trying to remember what the papers had meant, perhaps now he would understand.

Addy directed Adelaide to a place to park. "This is as far as the car can go," he said.

The trio walked the rest of the way. Raisin picked up a few wildflowers that had survived the summer heat and Adelaide stopped often to inspect unusual shrubs that interested her.

"We're almost there," said Addy, restlessly and then he laughed and ran ahead.

"What is it, Addy?" asked Aunt Adelaide. Raisin watched Addy toss some small rocks. Three rocks landed in the stream and Raisin jumped to avoid the splash and laughed, but Adelaide watched the boy's face sadden and she knelt down next to Addy.

A loose wad of papers crumbled in Addy's hands when he tried to lay the pieces out on the sand.

"It was a folder. It had some stuff 'bout me in it. I took it from the orphanage."

Adelaide placed a hand on Addy's shoulder.

"I don't think it's salvageable, son."

Addy wadded up the remains of the paper and tossed the rumpled ball into the stream.

"What was it you needed, Addy?" Raisin asked.

"It doesn't matter."

"I don't get it," persisted Raisin. "What was in the folder?"

"I don't know, okay?" Addy shouted. He started to stomp away, but stopped at Adelaide's request.

"Wait, Addy," said Adelaide, "let us help. We could go back to the orphanage."

"No," screamed Addy.

"Well, the police then," the aunt suggested.

"No. No," said Addy, turning away, "It's hopeless."

"Nothing's hopeless, Addy," Raisin said, stepping up to her friend.

"You're such a baby, Raisin. You think everything can be fixed. Well it can't. Maybe if I woulda been smarter, I coulda read it better, but I left it here to rot. I'm such a jerk."

When Adelaide started to console him, Addy moved away and ran through the woods. He was slumped over the car when they returned, but he was no longer crying.

The three of them munched on gingerbread cookies as the black Ford rattled back to Fever.

Chapter Seventeen

The Talent Show

"It's time Addy," Raisin yelled. "What are you doing in there?"

"I'm turnin' into a clown," said Addy smiling. Careful shopping at the Salvation Army had paid off. A large silk shirt rippled in the warm evening breeze like soft ice cream in the churner. Snapping the rainbow suspenders into place, Addy adjusted the baggy pants, remembering for a minute the night he had dug them out from the pile in Barley's office.

"Hurry up. Auntie has to be there early. We're leavin' without you," Raisin shouted.

"Perfection takes time, Anabelle, and I am going to be perfect tonight," Addy said, ignoring Raisin's last call from downstairs. With bright red lipstick, Addy drew two red patches to model rosy cheeks and another to imitate the expected "clown look" of a red nose. His long sloppy leather shoes clumped as he crossed the floor to the mirror and he squashed the half-eaten straw hat down over his ears. The result was exhilarating.

"Presenting." said Addy, imitating the professional tone of a ringmaster, "Barnum and Bailey's newest addition to clown alley..." Addy swooshed through the door and leaped into the hallway as he finished his introduction, "Baggy, the Clown!"

The hall was empty. The house was quiet.

"Oh, they really did leave. What a debut,"

said Addy, undaunted.

"The house is empty, but the show must go on." Addy clumped down the stairs and grabbed a biscuit from the bread box before he walked across the porch in search of his adopted family.

"Hello?" No one answered. Carrying the over-sized shoes, Addy began his walk to the school, which was easier in bare feet.

Once in sight of town, it was clear that the talent show was to be a big event and Addy's stomach began to feel like a large kettle of boiling oil. There were cars from other counties and unusual looking performers were signing up at a table. There was a long line.

For a moment, Addy was entranced. He must have been about seven when Barley took all the boys of the orphanage to the circus. An older boy was at the front of the line and all the little boys had to hold a cord to keep together. Barley disappeared and Addy had wandered into the tent to get closer to the clowns and the animals and the smell of the circus. He sat on the ground right in front of the circus until it was over. When he found the other boys outside the tent, Barley was back and he was drunk. The older boy took quite a beating for losing track of Addy.

"Here I am, Addy," said Raisin, running up to Addy with whipped cream on her fingers. "I had to help Auntie carry the pies. Sorry. You look wonderful. I think you're the only clown act tonight. What are you going to do?"

Addy didn't answer.

"Addy, are you all right?"

"Raisin, did ya see...like a group of boys...little boys...with a big scruffy guy?"

"You mean Barley? Why would he be here,

Addy?"

"Nah, that's stupid. He'd never bring the boys to a talent show. I was just thinkin' 'bout this time at a circus..."

"What about your act, Addy. Watcha gonna do?"

Addy took a deep breath to forget about the orphanage, "You'll just have ta wait and find out."

"Go sign up, Addy. I'll be watching."

"Wait, Raisin. Tell me where I go," Addy said, feeling a little confused and suddenly embarrassed.

"After they put you on the list, you go in the back door to the school to wait. The front porch on the school will be the stage, so I'll be sitting on the ground outside, right in the front row." Raisin gave Addy a "thumbs up" for success before she ran off to join her aunt.

In his mind, Addy listened to the roar of the lions, the music of the band, the roll of the drums, and the cheering of thousands of people as he walked up to the table. This would be his first night with a real audience. He was terrified in a vicarious sort of way, as if he was feeding off the excitement and gathering more energy all the time as each minute brought the moment closer.

A girl in a sailor dress and white tap shoes turned to stare at Addy.

Addy bowed low and introduced himself, "Baggy, the Clown, ma'am." Then he wiggled his big toe through a hole in his shoe and jumped to one side in fright. The girl screeched then smiled softly at the free entertainment.

"Get back in there. Bad toe," said Addy pounding his shoe with a fist. A set of blond twins crept closer to watch, covering their giggles with small pudgy hands.

Then it happened – Addy's worst nightmare.

A Buick sputtered into the school yard. The doors opened. A fat old man sucking on a cigar hiked up his pants as he scooted a group of boys into place at the back of the crowd. Like lightening splitting an oak, Addy was transformed – the moment he heard Barley's voice. He was afraid again, for his life, for the other boys. Afraid of getting caught and going back to Wood's Home.

Instantly, instinctively, Addy lowered his head and turned away, crawling to the security of the bushes that lined the garage. He watched Barley walk through the crowd. Somehow, Barley must have heard Addy was here. If Barley knew, he'd probably told everyone. The sheriff, the people running the talent contest...and Addy had almost signed up. They would have caught him for sure. Addy felt panicked. What will Raisin do if she sees the orphans?

From the back pocket of a large gentleman, Barley neatly pulled out a leather wallet. Addy drew in a breath and then covered his mouth to conceal himself. A thief, he thought to himself. He's picking people's pockets.

No sooner was the wallet in Barley's coat pocket than he had another. As the head of the school introduced the program, Barley worked his way through the crowd, bumping into people and apologizing and lifting whatever he could in the process.

Addy was worried about Adelaide and Raisin. He wanted to warn them, to protect them, but there was Barley, moving through the audience like a snake in the grass. Addy watched Barley wipe the side of his greasy face with a sleeve. He remembered that look. Barley was going drinking.

73

He had come to drop off the orphans, pick up some cash, and get drunk, but if Addy reported him, he would have to face him. And Barley would win. Then he'd take Addy back to the home and in front of the other boys he'd beat him. The feeling of Barley's hands around his throat made Addy so sick, he had to look away.

Barley had him and he didn't even know it. If Addy didn't show up for his act, Raisin and Adelaide would say something. If he did the act, the orphans would recognize him. He had to leave the only home he'd ever known.

Running, without the shoes, Addy let the tears fall, all the way to the house. He quickly removed the outfit and makeup and dressed for travel. He filled a pillowcase with his clothes, his precious belongings he had earned through his own labor. He scooped the rest of the biscuits into his bag and looked for paper. On a used envelope left at the table, Addy scrawled out a message.

der ante and Anabell. thank u for this huse and fud and close. i dunt want to go bac to WOODS HOME so i am leavin before i git kot. you are my bes frends. lov AddY.

Chapter Eighteen

Glendale

There was a circus coming to Glendale in August and it must be almost that time, Addy thought. But this was not the way he had imagined it, not like a thief, not the way he had left Wood's Home.

Thoughts whirled in Addy's mind. As much as he knew the flight north was inevitable, he wanted to run to Aunt Adelaide and ask her to hold him. Addy thought about the farm, the laughter they had shared. And then he thought about Barley and the people who always came to the orphanage to make their big legal decisions. Perhaps Adelaide and Raisin would be in trouble for keeping him. It was better if he left without speaking to anyone, but he would have to pass Fever to head north.

It was dark and the show had barely begun, so Addy decided he had time to take one more look at the crowd. The lights were lit around the makeshift stage and eyes were focused on a group of children, singing and square dancing. Addy skirted the town and stayed in the darker shadows of the empty stores and leafy trees that lined the wide street of town. With a firm stance on the base of the statue in the park, Addy could see the heads of everyone in the audience. Raisin was up front with Aunt Adelaide, just as she had said she'd be.

"I'm sorry," Addy whispered. His throat tightened and he wanted to cry. Quickly, he brushed the feeling aside. He pictured Raisin finding the note on the kitchen table. He wondered what Aunt Adelaide would say.

"Please don't be mad," Addy said, again in a whisper. Scanning the crowd, Addy recognized some of the people from Fever and many he had never seen before. Barley's half-cocked hat and grinding jaw sent a cold chill down his back when his eyes settled on the unmistakable form, looming over the seated bodies of some fifteen small boys. He looked restless and only partly drunk. Because he was still watching the crowd rather than the show, Addy wondered if Barley perhaps had heard Addy was here or was he just up to more of his mischief. Addy felt lucky to have escaped when he did.

Fifteen bowl-shaped haircuts and fifteen flour-sack shirts sat transfixed as they watched the stage. One of those boys was probably Skunker, but it was too dark to see and Addy was too far away. In his mind, he could picture Skunker smiling at the show from ear to ear, collapsing his freckles one upon another. The memory would have to do. He had to go...now.

Black-laced leather shoes carried Addy silently across the mowed grass and up the road. It took much less time to reach the familiar split-rail fence where he had once ducked into the corn in fear. Addy passed the fence, breaking again into a jog, breathing slowly and methodically as he ran.

When he was too tired to jog, he walked. When he was too tired to walk, he slept. When he awoke, he ate, and then it began again. He drank whenever he found water. He hid whenever cars could be heard or their dust trails signaled their approach. Not one person questioned him. Why should they? Addy figured he looked as respectable as the next person: pants, shirt, hat, shoes – well, maybe not the pillow case.

Cars began to pass more frequently and farms lined up so close together, a man could see his neighbor's wash on the line. There was no need to hide and food was easy to find among the many gardens and beautiful orchards of the Glendale valley.

The bright colors of a circus poster lured Addy in like a fish on a line. CECIL BRADY'S AMAZING FEATS OF FEARLESS FLIGHT the poster read. Performers encircled the words with their acts of twirling and leaping. A whitefaced clown tipped a black hat in one corner and a lion pawed the air in the other corner, causing Addy to take a cautious step back as the all-too-familiar breath still warmed his face when he thought back to the night he had hung by his collar, pressed against the bars of the tiger's cage.

The yellow and white striped tent and string of flags were not hard to spot, once Addy reached the large village. Rows of peaked roofs and streets squared off like lattice work, leaving the smell of fruit and flowers behind. A complex system of traffic passed him by from every direction. It was as if he didn't exist and this brought Addy a sense of safety. Addy felt hopeful as he looked over the size of the operation. This circus would be easier to join; it was bigger and surely there were many chores to do.

"You want the office, kid?" a man asked as Addy stepped across the border into the magical land of "circus people."

"Yes, sir," he answered, squaring his shoulders to appear as stout as possible.

"It's the red wagon, there," said the man, pointing down a row of railroad cars.

"Great. Thanks," Addy replied, but it was the

silent muscled back of a man carrying a bale of hay who failed to return his reply. Things were looking up though, Addy thought. It's a circus train. They're big and besides...I'm perfect...I'm ready.

Chapter Nineteen

Circus Time

The two iron steps up to the door of the office were the hardest stairs Addy had ever climbed. Not because they were high, but because suddenly there wasn't enough time to plan what he was going to say.

"Hi, I'm Addison Ray," he said, practicing the words over to himself. The door burst open and Addy crammed himself up against the railing to avoid collision with a fat woman whose scented scarves and rattling beads gave the impression a freight train of perfume was passing.

"Alrighta, Mista Brady. I donna wanna upset Tanzina. I talk to the man. I do it your way." The fat along the woman's arms wiggled as she shook her hands in the air in frustration. A man in a tan shirt and khaki shorts came to the door. He had a dark bushy mustache which matched his eyebrows.

With a frown of disgust, he looked at Addy and growled, "What do you want?"

"A job."

Three lines furrowed even deeper over the man's nose when he spattered out a grunt of "Ach" and flipped the door shut in Addy's face.

Without hesitation, Addy pushed in the door, just missing Mr. Brady's heel.

"I'm a clown. I have a stunt...an act...

"Oh yeah?" Mr. Brady's chair groaned as the short stocky ringmaster leaned back behind a desk suffocating under piles of papers.

"I follow a string of clowns under the big top. They're all sprayin' me with squirt guns. The band is playin'..."

"I know, kid. I been there. Get to the point."

Addy was sweating, but his energy was rising like a wildfire.

"Outta nowheres a horse comes flyin' inta the ring. The crowd screams in terror. A girl clutches the back a the horse. The clowns scatter. I races across the ring. I'm loosin' clothes. All I have left is a pair of baggy britches and bright suspenders." Addy jumps up on a chair and snaps a pair of imaginary suspenders.

"I leap up ta the wires, drop into the net, vault onta the back of the horse and saves her life. She gets down and bows, but I falls off and the horse runs over me. The clowns carry me out on a stretcher, but I jumps up and squirts 'em all with a water pistol 'cause I was fakin' it."

"Yeah, sure. Sounds great, but..."

"I can even do it without the horse," Addy said, hoping not to lose the attention of the ringmaster.

"But I don't need no clowns. I need a sweeper. So, you want the job?"

"Sweeper?"

"Yeah, like with a broom?"

"Yes, sir. Maybe later I could show ya..." The door burst open again and Addy jumped as if waking from a dream.

"Ralph, take this kid to Charley and tell him he's the new sweeper. Here, kid, fill this out and sign it," said Mr. Brady. "You got folks?"

"No, Sir."

"Good."

80

Chapter Twenty

Show Time

Charley kept Addy busy all day sweeping and cleaning up the grassy aisles in preparation for the public. The three rings in the tent had to be cleaned and painted. Wires were checked, performers practiced their acts, men argued and children silently obeyed. Time passed for Addy as naturally as if he had been a sweeper all his life.

When it came time to eat, Charley handed Addy a tin bowl of soup and a hunk of bread and told him to eat outside.

"Only the performers eat inside the tent," he said.

The bowl of soup wasn't enough to fill his belly completely, but Addy ignored the urge to ask for more and wandered off to explore the many tents and displays.

The animals looked healthy and the people working with the horses seemed very gentle. A man in overalls, his face half done in whiteface, brushed past.

"Sir?" Addy asked, "Could you tell me where clown alley is?" Addy liked knowing the words to use. He wandered into the tent the clown had pointed to and looked at the row of trunks and water buckets. It was set up just like the first circus he had seen. It won't be long, thought Addy, before I have a trunk in here.

From a trunk halfway down the alley, bold letters TILLII caught his eye.

"Tilly," said Addy and he ran to the trunk and looked around, but there was no one in sight. When he rushed outside the tent, Charley hailed him.

"It's gettin' close ta show time. Get to the ring and pick up papers, droppins, whatever it takes to keep the place clean. Don't let me catch you lolligaggin' around again."

"I'm on my way." said Addy, "Charley, do you know Tilly?"

"Tilly?"

"Yeah, the clown,"

"Oh, Lorenzo. He's pretty good. Cecil was lucky to get him."

"Lorenzo?" Addy about leaped out of his skin. Lorenzo was the name on that third paper in his file. Come to think of it, the whole name might be right. T.I.L II. That's what was on Tilly's trunk. The initials for the man in his file. His father?

"Oh my gosh," said Addy.

"What's wrong kid?"

"The name Lorenzo, it's..."

"It's what?"

Charley looked at Addy's dumb stare for a minute before cuffing him above one ear. "Get back to work, you lazy good-for-nothin'..."

Once inside the big tent, Addy was too busy to think about Tilly or Lorenzo, whatever his name was or if he was maybe his father. People had dropped their garbage everywhere. The music began and Addy's heart swelled with pride as the parade circled the arena. Dodging the elephants and horses to pick up manure was fun and he started to add a little clowning to his work, but Charley saw him and nodded a stern "NO" to reprimand him from a distance.

When a boy teased Addy about picking up a

load of horse droppings, Addy just smiled and said, "Yeah? How many people do you know who work for Cecil Brady's Circus?"

"This circus ain't nothin'," said the boy, "Ringling, Barnum and Bailey Circus gots a hundred train cars and their own private home in Florida. They even got Tom Mix, the cowboy. He makes ten thousand bucks a week. What do you make?"

"Probably more than you do," said Addy in defense although the sting of the boy's words had cut into him a little.

Mr. Brady bumped into the boys just long enough to curse Addy and break up the fight.

Charley caught up with Addy at the far end of the tent where he was slamming the broom across the floor in short hard strokes.

"Don't pay the brat no mind, Addy," said Charley. "You're a trouper now." In answer to Addy's questioning glance, Charley added, "That's circus talk. Means you're one of us."

"Charley," Addy asked, "Have you seen Tilly?"

"Look kid, forget about Tilly. For one thing, ya got Brady watchin' ya and he'll can ya if he catches ya messin' around. And second, Tilly. He likes ta be left alone. Lost his wife and kid in a fire and..."

"He did?"

The cymbals of the band crashed and the drums beat out a new jungle rhythm as the lions and tigers were rolled into place just outside the center ring. Charley left and Addy, still pondering over what Charley had said, listened. The sound of the band and the cheering of the crowd made Addy's skin creep in excitement and he moved closer. To avoid another reprimand, he continued to pick up bits of garbage in front of the viewers.

A man, naked to the waist, took his bows inside a huge cage in the center ring. As he snapped a long whip, the lions entered and leaped to their assigned seats. The music continued and clowns meandered around the path in front of the spectators to increase the tension of the audience as people "oohed" and "aahed" at each growl.

Ralph, Mr. Brady's assistant appeared behind Addy and leaned one arm on Addy's shoulder as if Addy should stand there and support him. "That darn Rolly."

"What's a matter?" Addy asked leaning on his broom to hold up Ralph's weight. Addy listened to Ralph, but he watched in fascination as one lion refused to take his seat.

"Rolly's the lion on the floor. Sometimes he's a pain and won't cooperate. Tanzina may just send him back to his cage after he plays it up a bit."

"Tanzina?"

"Yeah, the guy with the whip. He's a mean son of a ..."

Across the ring, the clowns were moving in for a closer look. The lion took his eyes off the whip and lunged at the side of the cage nervously when Mr. Brady started to relay a message to the trainer at the gate. Addy watched as Mr. Brady motioned angrily to Tanzina.

The lion disliked the confusion and tried to escape by crawling up the bars of his enclosure. When the cat hooked the claws of one paw in the netting at the top, he spun around and pulled one shoulder out of its socket.

The trapped beast cried out in a roar of pain, causing the seated cats below to panic and scramble around the floor. People everywhere were screaming, but circus performers streamed in from the exits to calm them down. Addy didn't know which way to turn. He wasn't afraid to be near the ring, but there was no one to tell him what he should be doing, so he turned to watch the lion.

Wildly, it ripped at the netting to free itself, only tangling its forearm worse in the woven net. The attendants worked quietly and systematically to usher the four lionesses back out the gate into their waiting cages.

Positioned ready at the trainer's exit, Mr. Brady raised a long black gun at the lion while Tanzina screamed at both the lion and the ringmaster from inside the cage.

"Don't shoot, Cecil," he yelled, "Rolly's caught. He's frightened. Wait."

When two other clowns trotted up to the lion's cage, Addy dropped his broom and ran to the scaffolding that supported the net. Someone may have yelled at him to stop, but there was so much noise, it was hard to tell. Addy wasn't thinking. This was the life he wanted to live and something inside told him he should be closer.

Once at the other side of the arena, Addy recognized Tilly. He was going to shout out to him, but at that instant, the lion ripped through the net at the top of the cage and pulled himself over the edge of the cage into the arena. One front leg wobbled at a strange angle as the lion crept through the sawdust toward Mr. Brady and his poised rifle.

The roar of the crowd became a deafening waterfall that drowned out the band, the painful growls of the wounded cat, and the argument of the men. In the slow motion of a dream, Addy turned and reached out with his arms toward the safety of the crowd. He closed his eyes and screamed, leaving the ring, the gun, the cat, and the clowns behind him.

The gun fired and Addy stopped. The crowd, still pushing toward the exits was hushed for a moment. The lion crouched in fear. Tanzina had raised the rifle's snout to save his lion and the bullet had only grazed the lion's ear, enraging the beast all the more. He snarled and roared and began again to slink his way toward the men. The people resumed their panicked escape and continued to scream.

Tanzina pushed Mr. Brady aside and yelled to his cat as he stepped back into the animal's path. Clowns moved in from all directions following the slow patient cues of Tanzina. They tried to herd Rolly back into the cage.

The frightened cat would have none of it. He bolted to one side and swatted at the closest moving target, Tilly.

Tilly's long shoes were flapping against the pavement as he ran for safety, but the lion was too quick. Ignoring the pleas of his trainer, the lion left the ground on three legs and pounced on the clown, who had only just reached a ladder.

"Tilly," Addy screamed. He felt his mouth open, but he could not hear the word. He could not hear the crunch of the lion's teeth bearing down into his friend's shoulder, but he could feel the pain.

"No," Addy screamed. With flailing arms Addy turned back into the ring and raced in front of the lion, still crouched over the victim, its jaws encircling its prey. From a corner of his eye, Addy could see blood pooling in the dust next to the clown. Gripping a support wire, Addy swung up into the net. The lion loped after him. Addy could hear the lion's breath gurgling from its own saliva as its sides heaved. They were both afraid.

From the net, Addy sprang to the ladder just

inches away from the claws of the cat, its wounded forearm still swinging miserably at its side. The cat reached with one outstretched paw and jumped at Addy. With its lips drawn back, the lion hissed and bared its wet white teeth. A shot rang out and echoed as the audience, all at once, sighed with relief. Addy could hear the lion fall into the net. He could hear his own blood pumping wildly in his ears and when he was sure he had heard the lion fall, Addy looked down.

The lion's blood was dripping onto Tanzina, who stood just below the cat. The trainer grabbed a handful of fur in one hand and shook the still-smoking rifle in anger with the other. While tears streaked the tan face of the lion tamer as he bowed his head over his lion, Addy's tears began to flow as well. Slowly, still stiff with fear, Addy climbed down the ladder to kneel next to his friend.

Two clowns rolled Tilly onto a stretcher. For a moment Tilly opened his eyes. He looked into the face of his rescuer and smiled.

"Hi, Baggy," Tilly said, wincing as someone pressed a towel against his wound and the old man's face flushed in pain.

"Tilly," said Addy, "don't die."

"You got heart, kid."

"Tilly?" Addy cried, but the men brusquely pushed him aside to carry the stretcher to a waiting ambulance.

Mr. Brady took Addy by the arm and marched him out to the center of the arena. The ringmaster asked the audience to resume their seats and thanked them for their understanding. Addy assumed he was being held captive for his disobedience, like a prisoner, but he was too tired to resist.

Blindly, through a veil of tears, Addy watched the crowd stand and cheer as Mr. Brady thanked him for his bravery. He raised Addy's arm as he yelled, "heroically, with no concern for his own safety, Addison Ray, the youngest clown in the history of the Brady Circus, has saved the life of one of the most famous clowns in history...Timoteo Lorenzo the Second! Tilly..."

Addy didn't hear the rest. The name didn't sound right, although he couldn't remember exactly what it should have been. Everything had happened so fast today and he felt tired. He shouldn't be tired though. He hadn't walked fifty miles and he wasn't starving anymore, but his legs felt weak, like at the orphanage, when he had dragged his feet through the soft manure in the cow paddock.

"I have to go," he said to Mr. Brady who was still calming the crowd with his words of authority when Addy walked out the exit in search of the ambulance. It was gone. The clowns were gone. Performers were lining up for the next act as if nothing had happened.

Chapter Twenty-one

August First

"It's August first, Addy," said Charley. "We move out after the last show and set up in Hartford at dawn. "Cecil says ya can add your act and sweep at the same time."

"It's about time," said Addy.

"Now get up and get to work."

From his bunk atop four bales of hay, Addy squinted to finish his letter in the dull light. "I'm writin' my Aunt Adelaide a letter."

"I thought ya said ya didn't have no family."

"She ain't really an aunt. She's more like a ma and Raisin lives there, the girl I told you about that wants to be a bareback rider. Her ma died ridin' though and I don't think her aunt wants her to do it."

"She your girl?" Charley asked, poking Addy in the ribs with his broom.

Addy smiled, to himself, high on his bunk, where no one could see him.

"Naw, she's just a girl."

"You comin' down from there."

"Nope. I still gotta write Skunker and I don't write so good. It takes me awhile. I'm not even sure he gets these letters."

"Oh yeah, the runt at the orphanage."

Addy dropped his pencil and leaped on Charley and wrestled him to the ground.

"He ain't no runt."

Charley was laughing so hard he couldn't

answer, but when he got his breath he pinned Addy down and apologized. "Okay, Mr. Baggy Britches, he ain't no runt. Now you gonna get your wimpy little butt to work or do I have to knock out a few of those pretty teeth of yours?"

The circus was Addy's family now and Charley was his brother. He accepted Charley's orders and respectfully grabbed his broom.

"Oh yeah, one more thing."

Addy turned and narrowed his eyes, expecting Charley to heap some more chores on his already busy schedule.

"Tilly's comin' back today."

With that, Addy straightened and jumped right up to Charley's face, "How is he?"

"His arm and collar bone are broken and he's pretty weak, but the boss says he's fit enough to travel and stay on the train."

"Can I go see him, Charley?"

"Naw, he'll see ya when he gets back. Don't you go pesterin' him none though. From what I hear, he's lucky to be alive on accounta he lost so much blood."

For hours, Addy worked meticulously through the aisles between tents, cleaning and carrying bales of hay to each wagon. With so much to think about – the name he couldn't remember in the file, his new act, Tilly, traveling on a train – it was a surprise to Addy when Charley told him to wash up for supper and put on a clean shirt.

"What for, Charley? I never noticed you carin' much about smell."

"You stink and I don't want the boss yellin' at me that my charges smell worse than the animals. So do it," Charley said, smiling. Addy was suspicious, but pulled a clean shirt from his pillowcase and strutted to the wash basin obediently.

Clean and refreshed, Addy walked to the mess tent for supper. A hand-scrawled sign announced dinner and an all-circus meeting next to the train. When he arrived at the back of the crowd, the circle opened. A wall of smiling faces and open arms ushered him into the center where a smaller number of chairs half-encircled a table covered with gifts. There, propped up like a hot dog in a bun, sat Tilly, nestled in a blanket.

All Addy could say was, "Tilly," before the entire company burst out with a chorus of "Happy Birthday." From Tilly's shining face, Addy eyes drifted to the table, to the cards labeled with the names Addy, Addison, or Baggy, and to the next chair where Mr. Brady sat singing out the lines as heartily as the rest.

Seated next to him was the graceful figure of Aunt Adelaide.

"What're ya doin' here?" Addy asked. Adelaide smiled and clasped her hands in her lap as she always did. Raisin stepped in behind her singing loudly out of tune and then Addy turned as someone short tugged at his pant's pocket.

"Skunker," Addy said in surprise, looking deeply into the dark chocolate eyes of his long lost buddy. He was going to ask Skunker how he got there too, but the song stopped and Addy put his hands in his pockets and pressed his lips together tightly to keep from crying.

"Speech," yelled the crowd, but Addy was dumbstruck, unable to think clearly, unable to put together words or understand how this had come to be.

"I didn't know it was my birthday," Addy said

shyly.

His circus friends laughed.

"Well, I have something to say," said Aunt Adelaide. Adelaide rose and stepped out to face the crowd and put one arm across Addy's back. "I haven't known Addison long, but he took me on a journey one day: a journey into his past. We found a file in the woods, his file he had hidden from the orphanage, but it was soaked clear through. Whatever information about Addy's life had been in there, was ruined.

"But I've been doing some checking..."

Addy looked at Tilly and smiled. He knew what she was going to say. It had to be true.

"I didn't want to raise Addy's hopes, but I drove to the town of Copperstock to look into the police files for Addison's records.

"It seems he was abandoned in a park there as a baby and the police took him to the local orphanage," said Adelaide, glancing over at Addy, who tucked his head in embarrassment. "When he was ten, Addison was assigned to the man running the home for permanent foster care. The man just used Addy to run his farm because he knew the child had a strong back and an obedient nature."

"Auntie, please," Addy begged.

"It's all right, Addy, I'm almost done, but not everything I have to say will be pleasant. A year later, a man came to the police station to attempt to regain custody of this child, but failed."

Addy's sparkle turned to glaze. Almost equal in height, he searched Adelaide's eyes and soft face for hope.

"I'm afraid," Adelaide continued, "that the man was unable to provide a birth certificate or knowledge of the whereabouts of the mother.

Unfortunately, he was arrested that year and died
shortly after in a county jail." The crowd gave a sad
sigh in support of Addy's story. All eyes were on
Adelaide as she continued.

"There's more though," Adelaide smiled and
gave Addison a brief hug. "The night Addy left our
little town of Fever, the man who runs the
orphanage was caught picking pockets."

Addy smiled again and looked at Skunker.
His freckled face was pudgy and beaming as if he'd
been pumped full of air, like a balloon. Even Addy
had never seen him so happy. It suddenly occurred
to him that Skunker was here without other
orphans, without anyone from Copperstock.

Addy was about to interrupt when Adelaide
said, "Skunker was about to kick the old guy as the
police hauled him away..."

Everyone laughed and Skunker shrank back
behind Addy.

"...but," Adelaide continued, "the man called
him...well, he called him a bad name, and then he
said 'You little rat, you're as ungrateful as your
brother' and that's how we found out Addy had a
half-brother at the orphanage."

"Me," Skunker said, yanking on Addy's shirt,
"I'm your brother."

Addy looked at Skunker and Skunker
punched Addy gently in the arm like old times, but
Addy was too overcome to speak.

Raisin could no longer contain herself and she
burst out the rest, "And we adopted him, Addy. He's
gonna live with us and whenever you're not circusin',
you can too."

"I..well...thanks," Addy said, knowing it
wasn't enough. What do you say to someone who
has made things right, when you didn't think it ever

could be. Just when he thought he'd never have a real family, he had two: Adelaide and Raisin and Skunker, living in Fever, and the Circus, where he could be Baggy the Clown.

Mr. Brady broke Addy's awkward silence with his booming voice, "This is a heck of a cake. Let's eat." The performers gathered around the table while Addy knelt down next to Tilly.

Tilly pressed a large gentle hand to Addy's head and said, "I'm just an old fool, lad. I don't know how to be a pa. I came from Italy sixty years ago with nothin' and I ain't got more to my name now than an old trunk and...well, that's about it...but, if you'll have me, I..." Tilly couldn't finish, but the look Addy shared with him told him he didn't have to.

"I knew you was my pa the minute I saw ya," Addy said.

"Addy," Raisin broke in, "They put Barley in jail and Skunker said some new people come out to the orphanage to take it over."

"They're fixin' it up," Skunker said. "I got ta paint the fence. Ya know? The one ya use ta balance on."

"Yeah," said Addy, "I remember."

Addy turned and looked as Adelaide placed her hand on Skunker's shoulder and the little freckle-face nodded enthusiastically.

"Open your presents, lad," boomed Mr. Brady in his best ring voice, "We gotta circus ta run here." The performers cheered and sang a chorus of "He's a Jolly Good Fellow."

Raisin stood by the pile of presents and looked at Addy. She smoothed out the pressed apron over her pinafore and placed her brown braids neatly over each shoulder.

"Okay, Raisin," said Addy, "You pick." Raisin

94

fetched a present off the top of the table.

Addy ripped open the newspaper and string. A clown with a red nose, baggy pants and striped suspenders was smiling back at him with a forlorn-looking grin.

"Yeah," said Addy, "I like it. It's me."

"Addy," Raisin whispered close to her friend, "Will I ever see you again?"

Addy ran a finger around the figure of the clown and looked up at Raisin.

"Anabelle Lee," said Addy, "Ya gotta take care of Skunker for me." Raisin looked puzzled for a minute.

"'Cause when I get my own circus, I'm gonna need a bareback rider and a manager." They chuckled quietly. Skunker squeezed in between them and prodded Addy to open the rest of his gifts, but Addy placed the clown on the table and told his little brother he wanted to admire this one for awhile.

29813147R00059

Made in the USA
Charleston, SC
25 May 2014

THE C

*'If marriage is your objective I'd advise you
to steer clear of the medical profession,'*
surgeon Ross Noble warns Camilla
Clifton. But as a newly-qualified staff
nurse, filled with enthusiasm for her
profession, marriage is the last thing
on Camilla's mind. And if it weren't,
Ross Noble is the last man she'd consider
marrying.

THE
CLASSIC
SYMPTOMS

BY

GRACE READ

MILLS & BOON LIMITED
15–16 BROOK'S MEWS
LONDON W1A 1DR

First published in Great Britain 1985
by Mills & Boon Limited

© Grace Read 1985

Australian copyright 1985
Philippine copyright 1985

ISBN 0 263 75126 0

Set in 11 on 12½ pt Linotron Times
03–0985–45,000

Photoset by Rowland Phototypesetting Ltd
Bury St Edmunds, Suffolk
Made and printed in Great Britain by
Richard Clay (The Chaucer Press) Ltd
Bungay, Suffolk

CHAPTER ONE

THE FATEFUL day had at last arrived. That Monday morning Camilla was on early duty but Sister Hunter had said she could wait for the post. The previous night she had hardly slept a wink. Now she felt sick with dread as she thought about the possibility of failure. Letting out a tremendous sigh, she pulled a brush through her glossy red-gold hair and sighed yet again.

Marie, with whom she shared the first-floor flat, knelt on the window-seat, a velour dressing-gown wrapped around her comfortable curves. She peered out into the street. 'He's just coming down the road,' she said.

'Oh dear!' Camilla groaned. 'What'll I *do* if it's a fat envelope?'

One set ahead of Camilla in her training, Marie had passed the Finals hurdle and was now a staff nurse, entitled to wear the coveted frilled cap. She knew all about the agony of waiting for the SRN results. A thin envelope would spell success; a fat one signified failure and the enclosure of an entry form for a resit.

'Drink your coffee,' she said calmly. 'I'm sure you've made it. If not there's no justice in this world, with all the work you did.'

Having been blessed with a photographic memory, Marie could conjure the page of a textbook at will and had done hardly any revision herself. Camilla did not share her confidence, especially since at the time of her exam she had just split up with Tony Sinclair, one of the housemen.

It was not until he was leaving to take up another appointment in the North that he'd broken it to her he was getting engaged to a girl he'd known in medical school. Camilla was over him now. She accepted that the affair had been just a pleasant diversion for him while he was at St Martin's. But at the time she had been badly hurt and her concentration for the all-important exam had wavered.

The click of the letterbox told her that the postman had delivered their mail. She covered her face with her hands. 'Oh gosh! Will you go down . . . I daren't look.' Her heart pounded violently as Marie skimmed downstairs.

A minute later her friend came bounding back, whooping with delight and brandishing the thin buff envelope.

'I did it?' Camilla ripped open the envelope and read the wonderful words . . . *We have much pleasure in informing you* . . . 'I did it!' she squealed, half laughing, half crying. 'Oh, I can't believe it.'

The two girls hugged each other and danced around the room.

'Well, thank goodness for that. Now I can go back to bed and finish my beauty sleep,' said Marie.

She was on a day off. 'See you later. I'll meet you in The Friars this evening and we'll celebrate.'

'Okay. Now I must get a move on.' Camilla could hardly wait to get to the hospital to share her good news and hear how the rest of her set had fared. Packing a clean uniform into her holdall, she slipped a lightweight rain-jacket over her check shirt and jeans and set off for work on winged feet.

It was a morning to beat all mornings, bright with May sunshine. So far the traffic was comparatively light. Soon pavements, trains and buses would be thronging with the capital's workers, but for the moment the awakening city had time to breathe. Plane trees were in new green leaf and even the sparrows could be heard chirruping.

Joining the trickle of early-birds at the Underground, Camilla grinned at the ticket collector who cast a lustful eye over her trim hips and gave her a cheeky wolf-whistle. She felt like yelling to the world, 'I've passed!'

The journey to the City station and the illustrious teaching hospital of St Martin's took her roughly twenty minutes. She did have a small car—a twenty-first birthday present from her father—but she used it only for leisure. Hospital parking spaces were reserved for consultants and other VIPs, not for small fry like student nurses.

Going through the huge wrought-iron gates and into the shady square in front of the hospital, she was hailed by June Finch, one of the girls from her set. They greeted each other excitedly.

'Have you . . . ?' they both said at once, but knew they didn't really need to ask. The delight on their faces told all. They walked on together in radiant spirits.

'You've got a job here, have you?' Camilla asked.

'Yes, I'll be staffing on Neurology. What about you?'

'I'll be staying where I am, on Simpson.'

Pushing their way through the swing-doors and into the reception area, they stayed chatting elatedly for a moment before parting company.

Camilla made for the surgical block. As she neared the Senior Medical Staff Common Room a tall, well-dressed man emerged and glanced back casually in her direction before heading for the theatre wing.

Instinctively she slowed her pace, her lively green eyes widening. She had caught only a fleeting glimpse of his face but a distant memory surfaced. There was no mistaking that strong, square-jawed profile and the crisply-waving thick blond hair. It was Ross Noble . . . the doctor who had sent tingles down her spine and filled her with awesome respect during her first spell in Theatre as a very raw first-year.

Her gaze followed the upright, broad-shouldered figure until his leisurely stride took him out of sight. With vivid recall she saw herself flaking out in Theatre when she had witnessed her first operation. There had been the sudden lurch of her stomach as the laparotomy incision was made, followed by a draining of strength from her legs. She remembered Ross Noble's laconic, 'Catch her!' as her head started spinning.

Afterwards he had enquired with some amusement if she felt better. Camilla had spent the rest of her time in Theatre trying to remain as inconspicuous as possible, and not to look when the knife went in.

In the hospital newsletter there had been an account of his engagement to an attractive socialite. Shortly afterwards he had left St Martin's to go somewhere else. But he had remained tucked away at the back of Camilla's mind as her ideal of what a doctor ought to be. He was courteous to the nursing staff and kind to the patients. He'd had an infectious laugh, opening his mouth as he did so to show a set of slightly uneven but pearly teeth. She imagined half the female patients must fall for him.

After all this time Camilla doubted that he would remember her, the nervous little first-year who had made an ass of herself. She hoped not. It had been known that changes were imminent in Professor Purbright's team and she assumed that Ross Noble was to be the new senior surgical registrar.

In the locker room she changed into her blue and white striped uniform, arranged her navy-bordered cap on the back of her bright hair and savoured the moment when she would be exchanging it for the muslin and lace affair. But there was no time to dally when the calls of Simpson Ward awaited. She was already a little late, although with permission. Sister Hunter ran her ward with brisk efficiency and today was theatre day, which would keep them all on their toes.

The early morning shift were still gathered in the office where Night Staff Nurse Matty Newbury had just finished reading her report. Everyone glanced up when Camilla appeared in the doorway.

'Good morning, Sister, sorry I'm late,' she said, her eyes sparkling.

Jean Hunter smiled expectantly. 'Well?' she said. 'I don't think we need to ask, do we?'

Camilla grinned. 'I made it!'

Exclamations of delight surrounded her and she was patted on the back and congratulated by them all.

After a while Sister Hunter brought them down to earth. 'Save the celebrating till later or we shall get behind.' Her pleasant grey eyes flitted over the staff. She was a tall woman in her late thirties with an air of confidence about her. Her dark blue dress was always immaculate and her thick dark hair neatly French-pleated beneath the flowing tails of her cap. 'Avis, do something about your hair before you start work,' she went on, 'you can't have it flopping about like that.'

'Yes, Sister.' Second-year student Avis Riley pushed the offending slippery brown locks behind her ears and repinned them under her cap.

Tasks were appropriated to various nurses and the orderly routine of the day began.

To Camilla came the responsibility of ensuring that the patients for surgery were prepared in good time for their call to theatre. Heading the list was Miss Rose. She was a large lady, headmistress of a girls' school. It was her first experience of being in hospital and Camilla guessed it was something of an ordeal for the refined spinster. Her pre-medication having been given by the night staff, Camilla went to check that everything was as it should be.

Miss Rose opened anxious pale blue eyes at the movement of the bed curtains. 'Hallo, dear,' she said. 'Is it time?'

'No, not quite, Miss Rose. I just came to see if you were okay. You've had a bedpan, haven't you?'

The patient nodded, her forehead furrowed with anxiety. 'It's very much a case of *Your Life in Their Hands*, isn't it? Is Professor Purbright good at this kind of thing?'

'Oh yes, he's very well thought of.'

'But not very forthcoming. I had to ask the other doctor the things I wanted to know.'

'Who was that?'

'A Mr Noble. He said he could foresee no problems.'

'Well, there you are then.' Camilla smiled reassuringly and checked that the identity bracelet was in place on her patient's wrist. 'Now you settle down and have a doze. I'll be going with you when the time comes, and before you know it you'll be back here in the ward.' She closed the curtains around Miss Rose's bed.

All washing bowls had by now been cleared away, beds finished and breakfasts were about to be distributed to those patients who were entitled.

Surveying her tidy ward, Jean Hunter clicked her teeth. 'Camilla . . . Mrs Brookes is not sitting out. Get her up, will you?'

Hilda Brookes had had her gall bladder removed a week previously and was resisting all attempts to get her moving. 'Come along, Hilda,' said Camilla cheerfully. 'You'll enjoy your breakfast much more sitting out.' She reached into the patient's locker and found her dressing-gown and slippers.

'Oh—must I?' whined Mrs Brookes. 'I feel as weak as a kitten.'

'Yes, I know. But it's better for your chest. If you lie around you're going to get bronchial complications, and you don't want that, do you?' Firmly she turned back the bedclothes and assisted the patient to a chair.

Hilda puffed and groaned. 'You're all heartless, you young nurses.'

'It's for your own good, Hilda.' Camilla pulled the bed-table nearer. 'There you are. We'll get you back again presently.'

The theatre porters came for Miss Rose. Camilla arranged the covers over her patient on the trolley. 'We're on our way,' she said in a soothing voice, gathering together case notes and X-rays. 'Soon be over now.'

'Take your coffee-break before you come back, Camilla,' Sister Hunter called as they left the ward.

Trundling the trolley along the corridor and into the lift, one of the porters was full of complaint. 'Flipping Purbright, dumped his yappy Yorkshire terrier in our lodge. His wife's away or summat, so we're expected to look after it while he's here.'

'Oh, they're nice little dogs, Yorkshire terriers,' Camilla said. 'Do you have any pets, Miss Rose?'

Miss Rose shook her head feebly. She was quite lethargic now and past caring about anything.

They arrived at the barrier to the Anaesthetics Room, where a theatre nurse took over the patient. Before the doors closed on the sterile zone Camilla had a brief glimpse of the figures beyond. Even dressed in his greens, with a cap over his fair hair, the stalwart figure of Ross Noble was clearly recognisable. Pushing through the doorway to the operating room, his long-lashed eyes above the mask glanced her way before he disappeared from sight. She felt there might have been recognition in that glance and thanked goodness she was no greenhorn now. Going on her way to coffee she was oddly pleased by his reappearance.

In the canteen a general air of excitement prevailed as everyone rejoiced with the new SRNs. Inevitably there were a few crestfallen students to be commiserated with, but their Clinical Tutor, who also put in an appearance, pronounced herself fairly pleased with the ninety per cent pass rate.

'The Completion of Training Service and

"Blessing of Caps" will be on Friday afternoon,'
she told them. 'Your parents are invited to attend.
I'll be putting full details up on the notice-board.'

Camilla glanced at her watch and decided she
just had time to telephone home. Quickly finishing
her drink, she left the others and hurried towards
the phones in the reception area. On the way the
rangy, white-coated figure of Casualty Officer
Julian Gilmore stopped her in her tracks. He had
been taking more than a passing interest in her of
late.

'Hi, Ginger! Do I gather from that Cheshire-cat
grin you have something to celebrate?'

Her grin broadened. 'Yes . . . I've qualified!'

'Great!' He looked her over, his eyes approving
her lissom figure. 'Now perhaps you'll have time to
spare to cheer up a depressed doctor.'

'Why? What are you depressed about?'

'All work and no play, sweetheart,' he returned
with a tragi-comic expression. 'Will there be
carousing in the Mess on Saturday?'

'I expect so.'

'Fine . . . we'll crack a bottle together.'

Camilla smiled. 'Must go, Julian. I've got a
phone call to make.'

Finding an empty booth, she dialled her home
number in Dorset. A male voice answered, a voice
she did not recognise. It wasn't her father, and it
didn't sound like Stephen Evans, his curate. 'Hallo,
is that the Vicarage?' she asked.

'Yep, but the Rev's not here.'

'Oh, well, is my mother there? Or my grand-mother? This is Camilla.'

'Hang about.'

Presently old Mrs Clifton's voice came over the wire. 'Camilla dear . . . how are you?'

'Over the moon, Gran. I just rang to tell you the good news. I've passed!'

'Oh, darling, that's wonderful! Congratulations! But then, we knew you would,' her grandmother added fondly. 'Sorry your parents aren't in . . . they'll be so thrilled.'

'Will you tell them there's a service on Friday when we get our new caps? They're invited if they'd like to come.'

'Friday . . . I'll look in the diary. Friday, oh dear. Your father has a meeting of the Synod that day and your mother's at the Juvenile Courts. Will I do?'

Camilla smiled ruefully. 'That's all right, Gran. It's a long way for you to come on your own.'

'Don't be silly. I wouldn't miss it for the world. I'll be there, barring a rail strike.'

'Okay, I'll put the details in the post. Who was that answered the phone just now?' Camilla went on.

'Oh, just a lad who's been having problems. He's staying here and doing a few odd jobs while they sort him out.'

Replacing the phone at the end of their conver-sation, Camilla felt grateful that she had a grand-mother. Sometimes it seemed as though her parents were shadowy characters whom she hardly knew. She had learned early in life the need to stand on her own feet. Coming home from boarding school for the holidays, she would find the vicarage occupied by various inadequate characters who might be in need of a refuge. Often she had been resentful of this invasion of her home life. It had certainly made her independent, but her grandmother had always been there, a sympathetic ear whenever she had needed one.

Now, of course, Camilla had her career and only occasionally went home. But nothing could dampen her spirits today. Back on the ward she continued on a high. The news had filtered through to the patients now and even the melancholy Hilda Brookes offered her congratulations.

Renewing a glucose/saline intravenous pack, Camilla was chatting light-heartedly to the patient when Sister Hunter came to find her.

'If you can come down from cloud nine,' she said with a tolerant smile, 'Miss Rose is ready for collection and you can deliver Mr Moore at the same time.'

Mr Moore was a small, cheerful little man who was due for a partial gastrectomy. Dopey though he was after his pre-medication, on the way to Theatre he even managed a joke about the housekeeping money his wife would save with having only half his stomach left to fill.

The same gloomy porter accompanied Camilla back to the ward with Miss Rose. 'Cor! The size of this one,' he grumbled, groaning as they transferred the inert bulk of Miss Rose to her bed. 'Hope you haven't got any more like her today, Nurse. You'll be 'aving me .in 'ere next with a rupture.'

'Oh, come on,' Camilla teased him, hanging the intravenous infusion bag on its stand, 'I'm only half your size and I'm yanking heavyweights up the bed all day long.'

With the help of Avis she arranged the covers over the sleepy patient. Then she checked pulse and respirations and made sure that the nasogastric tube was safely anchored. Miss Rose stirred and swallowed. 'Hallo, Miss Rose,' Camilla said, as the patient opened bleary eyes and blinked at her. 'It's all over, dear. You're back on the ward. Don't worry about the tube in your nose, it'll only be there for a little while. Everything's fine. Now you go back to sleep.'

Lunches were served, dressings done and routine procedures carried out. Visitors came and went. It was after tea before the operating team came to check on their cases. By this time Miss Rose was fully awake. She had been washed and put into her own nightdress and Camilla was about to aspirate the gastric tube. She paused when Sister Hunter brought Professor Purbright, Ross Noble and his assistant, Dr Lucy Greene, to the bedside.

Lucy was a diminutive young woman whose white coats were always too large for her. She was no pin-up, but she was a friendly person and respected by them all.

'Ah! Miss Rose, how are you feeling?' enquired Professor Purbright in benign tones.

The patient gave him a weary smile and eased herself carefully against the pillows. 'Not exactly full of beans, Doctor. Did you make a good job of me?'

A pleasantly unpretentious man, the professor's eyes twinkled and he stroked his long nose, glancing across at Ross Noble. 'Can you reassure the lady on that score?'

The registrar was head and shoulders taller than his senior, his healthy outdoors complexion contrasting with the paler looks of the consultant. 'Absolutely,' he said, a dimple flickering in one lean cheek. 'There were no problems. You were the perfect patient, Miss Rose.'

'Well, if your handiwork is equal to your bedside manner, you should go far,' she returned drily.

The professor chuckled. 'She can have pethidine four-hourly until she's comfortable, and she must have a chest X-ray tomorrow.'

Sister Hunter handed the registrar the medication chart on which he scrawled instructions for the analgesic.

Before the group moved on to the next patient, Ross Noble's compelling blue eyes held Camilla's for a moment and her colour heightened, a fact which was not lost on Miss Rose.

'I expect that young man causes a few flutters

among the nursing staff,' she remarked.

Camilla looked amused. 'Hospitals are not hotbeds of romance, Miss Rose. I'll get you your pain-killer in a minute, only Sister's got the drug keys in her pocket.'

The doctors left the ward. Camilla collected the keys from Sister Hunter and got Avis to check the prescription with her.

'Pethidine, fifty mgs . . . right?'

Avis referred to the chart. 'Crumbs! Is that what that's supposed to be?'

'Yes, shocking scribble, isn't it? He ought to be shot.'

'Who's that you'd like to polish off, Nurse?'

The deep voice behind her made her jump. She turned to find Ross Noble there, eyebrows raised equivocally.

'Well, you, I suppose,' she said with some embarrassment. But knowing she had a valid point, she met his eyes boldly. 'If I hadn't heard what Professor Purbright ordered I should have had to get you to confirm it. If doctors wrote legibly in the first place it would save a lot of trouble.'

He shot her a guarded glance from under his straight brows, took the sheet, produced a gold ball-point from the top pocket of his white coat and with elaborate care rewrote the prescription. 'Does that suit you?'

'That's fine,' she said. 'Now, can I help you?'

'I shouldn't think so, Nurse . . .' he paused, while his gaze travelled to the identity label pinned on her uniform, '. . . Clifton.' Then he walked away to Sister's office.

Avis giggled, looking after him. 'You were cool! Bet that shook him. Smashing though, isn't he? Looks like a lion with that gorgeous hair.'

Camilla made no comment. She snapped the top off the ampoule and drew up the drug into the syringe. It was odd, she reflected, how much more self-assured she felt, knowing that she was really qualified at last. Imperious doctors did not intimidate her now.

When she had given the injection to Miss Rose it was time for her to go off duty. Reporting to Sister Hunter before leaving, she found Ross Noble still in the office reading through some case notes. He rose, handed the folder back to Sister and followed Camilla out of the ward.

'I seem to know your face from somewhere,' he remarked, catching her up. 'Should I?'

'I was a first-year when you were here before.'

His eyes narrowed thoughtfully. 'You fainted in Theatre!'

'Yes, I'm afraid I did.'

'So you managed to stay the course. Less squeamish now?'

'Much.'

'And with much more to say for yourself than in those days.' A satirical smile twisted his generous mouth. 'I can see I shall have to watch my step on Simpson Ward in future.' He carried on walking and disappeared around the corner.

Camilla stopped by the lift and pressed the button. Her heart was pounding for some obscure reason. She discovered that she felt far from self-assured after all.

Changing out of uniform, she met up with some of the other new SRNs and they made a beeline for The Jolly Friars, a local patronised by the hospital staff. Marie was already there, as promised, having cancelled a date with her boyfriend, Luke, in favour of the celebrations.

'I suppose we'll have to be thinking about post-grad courses next,' said June Finch as they toasted their success. 'Anything in mind, Cam?'

She shook her head dreamily. 'I'm not thinking that far ahead yet. I'm happy to stay where I am for now. Jean Hunter's great to work with, and Prof Purbright's no problem.'

'Oh yes, and he's got that delicious new registrar, hasn't he?' someone else put in.

'Don't you remember him from when we first started here?' Camilla reminded them. 'I think he's changed though . . . something different about him . . . not so easy-going as he used to be. At least, that's the impression I got today.'

'Well, he's older for one thing,' said Marie. 'And he was all set to marry some society bird, wasn't he? Perhaps the social whirl has taken its toll.'

Other staff members drifted in to swell the crowd and celebrate with the successful students. Soon the low-ceilinged historic saloon bar was crammed to bursting point and resounded with good-

humoured raillery. But presently the party had
to break up. Apart from the ongoing life of the
hospitals, the City was a deserted place when
offices had closed for the night and public houses
shut earlier in consequence.

In the tube, on the way back to the flat, Marie
and Camilla chattered on blithely, although
Camilla found her thoughts constantly straying in
the direction of Ross Noble. His deep blue eyes
haunted her. They seemed to have a brooding
quality, almost an air of disillusionment, and there
was a sterner set to his chiselled lips.

Dealing with sickness and human tragedy day
after day was bound to have its effect, she supposed. Her own experience had taught her that.
Whatever defences you built for yourself, you
never became totally inured to other people's
suffering. Even when you were off duty it wasn't
always easy to forget the patients.

She pushed the intriguing registrar from her
mind and tried to concentrate on the pleasures and
pitfalls of being an SRN at last. On the one hand
there would be a rise in salary and, on the other
hand, more responsibility. But it was great to think
that, for the time being at any rate, exams were
behind her.

Later that night her father telephoned. 'Well
done, my dear. We're all proud of you,' he said.

She had never thought to hear him say that. He
was not given to praising her efforts. Even when
she had done particularly well at school, or passed a

music exam, or was made house captain, he had accepted it as a matter of course.

'So my presence is desired on Friday, I hear,' he went on.

'But I thought you couldn't come?'

'I shall make my excuses to the bishop. My daughter warrants precedence on this occasion, I think.'

Well! That was quite a concession from him. Camilla's cup was full.

Her mother came on to speak to her next. 'Yes, well done, Camilla, but I suppose it was a walkover for you,' she said blandly.

'No, it wasn't. I worked really hard.'

'Oh, come on, don't be modest. And what now? I always thought you should have done the thing properly and gone to medical school. I suppose it's not too late for that. Think about it.'

'No, Mummy . . . that's not me. I'd be useless. Besides, I like nursing.'

'Well, it's your life of course. Look, I'm sorry I can't support this Capping Service, but I have my duties to fulfil.'

Her mother's attitude did not surprise Camilla. She was used to it. But her father's reaction had really made her day. Actually putting his daughter before the bishop? Wow!

CHAPTER TWO

THE Completion of Training Service was held in the old and beautiful hospital chapel. A small gathering of relatives and hospital officials had assembled and awaited the arrival of the newly-qualified nurses. In uniform, but bareheaded, they filed into the front two pews. Camilla had come straight from the ward. Her eyes searched for and found her father and grandmother among the visitors. She exchanged smiles with them as she took her seat.

It was a simple but moving occasion during which the caps were blessed by the chaplain and placed upon the heads of the new SRNs. Feeling quite emotional, Camilla repeated with the others the Nightingale pledge to practise her profession faithfully.

The short service at an end, everyone was invited to take refreshments in the Sisters' Dining-Room, where they were welcomed in a gracious manner by the senior tutor.

Camilla found a tray and brought tea and cakes for her visitors. She was not a bit like her father, a dark-haired, solidly built man with angular features. She more resembled her grandmother, whose hair had also once been auburn but had now faded to a soft sandy colour.

'Ridiculous scraps of nonsense, those caps,' said the Reverend Philip Clifton, popping a dainty sandwich into his mouth. Despite the derisory comment, he eyed with satisfaction the seal of success on his daughter's bright hair.

'Tradition dies hard at St Martin's, Dad,' returned Camilla. 'Do you know they still keep leeches in the pharmacy here?'

'Good gracious!' her grandmother exclaimed. 'But they don't use them, do they?'

'Very occasionally. When I was in A & E they used one to reduce a haematoma on someone's eyelid.'

Old Mrs Clifton shuddered with distaste. 'Ugh! Change the subject or you'll put me off my tea.'

Camilla's father set down his cup, reached into the pocket of his clerical black jacket and handed her a small, flat jeweller's case. 'You'd better have this. I bought it some weeks ago in anticipation.'

Somewhat surprised, she opened it up to find a silver belt-buckle, oval in shape with an intricate design of leaves and flowers. 'Oh, Dad! That's absolutely gorgeous. Thank you.' Touched by the unexpected gesture, she reached up to kiss his craggy cheek.

He was not a demonstrative man, except in the pulpit where he performed to some effect. (Camilla often thought he would have done well as an actor.) Public displays of affection he found embarrassing. He patted her awkwardly on the shoulder. 'I supposed you'd be wanting one.'

They intermingled with other family groups. Introductions were made, pleasantries were exchanged with the nursing officers, and Camilla's father had a long talk with the chaplain.

After a while people began to leave and the Reverend Clifton glanced at his watch. 'Well, Mother, I think we should be moving too.'

'And I ought to get back,' Camilla said. 'Sister Hunter told me not to rush, so I can see you off the premises first. We're not that busy.'

She escorted them through the maze of corridors and across the leafy square towards the main gates. Several ambulances passed them on the way.

'More customers for you,' her grandmother said.

'That's something we're never short of,' laughed Camilla. 'Thanks for coming, both of you.'

'We don't see too much of you these days,' her father remarked. 'Why don't you come home on your next days off?'

'Okay, I'll try. Give my love to Mummy.' Kissing them goodbye, she waved them out of sight and walked quickly back towards the hospital buildings, feeling a little self-conscious in her new headgear.

Hearing footsteps and the sound of male voices behind her as she reached the entrance, she paused to hold open the door. She might as well have been invisible. Without the slightest acknowledgement, Ross Noble walked straight through with a houseman and the pair of them strode on, continuing their conversation.

'And thank *you*,' Camilla muttered with indignation. But her eyes lingered on the registrar's broad shoulders, admiring the set of them and the way his lustrous hair glinted as it moulded to the curve of his head. Then she took the lift to Simpson Ward.

When she reported back, Sister Hunter had just put down the telephone. 'Everything go okay?'

'Great!' said Camilla.

'Well, you can go and show off your new cap in A & E. They want to borrow someone. There's been a multiple road traffic accident and they're short-staffed. You're the best one to go since you know the ropes there.'

Camilla hurried back the way she had come. Ken Drew, the charge nurse with whom she had worked before going to Simpson, was coming from one of the treatment rooms. 'Well, well! Who's a clever girl then? I heard you were through.' He held out his hand and shook hers. 'Congrats, Cam.'

'Thank you, Kenny. I believe you wanted some help down here?'

He rolled his eyes. 'The understatement of the year! Be a pet and take over in Room Three, will you? Chap in there with a Pott's fracture and possibly cracked sternum. There's a second-year with him but she's new here, expect she'd appreciate some assistance.'

Going into Room Three, Camilla smiled at both patient and student. 'Hallo, I've been sent to help. How are you getting on?'

The casualty was a middle-aged man with dark hair silvering at the temples and, judging by the quality of his clothes, a man of affluence. There was a disquieting pallor about his clean-shaven cheeks and his well-kept hands looked limp and bloodless.

The junior seemed rather flustered, helping him off with his clothing. 'Oh, this is Mr Bolton, Staff. I've been asked to get him ready for X-ray. Wh-what . . . how do we deal with his trousers?'

Camilla sized up the situation and the swollen, fractured ankle which was resting on a pillow. 'We will have to cut the trousers off, I'm afraid. Sorry about that, Mr Bolton, but it's the only way to avoid hurting you and doing more damage.'

'Do what you like,' he sighed weakly.

Taking out her scissors, she began to slit up the seam on the side of his injured leg. 'Have you done his observations?' she murmured to the student.

'No, not yet.'

'All right, let's finish undressing him first.' Carefully easing off the trousers, Camilla covered his legs with a blanket and put him into an examination gown. Then she closed her fingers over his pulse. It was alarmingly fast and feeble and he was taking intermittent sighing breaths. 'What happened to you?'

'The van . . . in front of me braked sharply . . . it hit a pedestrian. I went into the back of the van . . . another car . . . ran into me . . .' He was finding it an effort to talk.

'I see.' Camilla caught sight of the pulsing vein in

his neck and suspected his injuries were more extensive than broken bones. She took his blood pressure. 'Mr Bolton, I think you'll feel better if we lie you down,' she said, lowering the head of the examination couch. 'Do you have pain anywhere else besides your leg and chest?'

'My dear, I hurt all over. I suppose that's not surprising. Er . . . I think I need to pass water.'

It needed no expertise, when he had made himself comfortable, to see that his urine was bloodstained. Leaving the junior to keep watch on him, Camilla went in search of a doctor. She found Julian Gilmore coming from the resuscitation room looking unusually solemn.

'Julian, can you spare a minute? I think the chap in Room Three should see someone quickly. His blood pressure's only eighty over sixty and there's frank blood in his urine; it could be kidney damage.'

'Okay. Nothing more I can do for that guy,' Julian said with a jerk of his head. 'Let's see what we can do for this one.' He followed her back into the room, made a full examination and asked the relevant questions.

'Well, Doctor, what's the verdict?' Mr Bolton made a feeble attempt at humour. 'I suppose I . . . shan't make my board meeting today?'

Julian gave a wry smile. 'I'm afraid not. I need to get someone else to see you, but I'm going to start you on a drip for now—your blood pressure's rather low.' He glanced across at Camilla. 'I'll take a blood test and put up some dextrose/saline.'

Camilla despatched the student to collect the infusion pack while she helped the doctor with the blood sample. When the drip was set up Julian disappeared to inform the surgical registrar while Camilla made out identity bracelets and attached them to Mr Bolton's wrist and good leg.

'Shall I be kept in?' he wanted to know.

'Almost certainly, I should think.'

He gave an involuntary shiver. 'It's so cold in here.'

It was actually quite warm in the department, but Camilla brought another blanket and tucked it around him. 'That better? You shouldn't have to wait too long,' she comforted.

Keeping a wary eye on him, she busied herself listing his belongings and putting them together in a plastic bag. In due course Julian returned with Ross Noble.

'Hallo, sir,' said the registrar, his practised eyes already assessing the patient. 'May I take a look at you?' Having been already briefed on the facts by Julian, he lifted back the blankets and gently palpated here and there, carefully noting the patient's reaction. Watching the proceedings, Camilla marvelled that such large, capable hands could be so sensitive.

'We think it's possible you have some kidney damage as well as the fractured ankle,' Ross said at length, replacing the covers. 'We ought to take a look inside you, and I think we should do that as soon as possible, if I may have your consent?'

'I'm in your hands,' said Mr Bolton.

'When did you last eat?'

'Not since lunch-time, about one . . .'

'Nothing since? Good.' The registrar nodded at Julian. 'Right, I should get the mobile X-ray along here. You have cross-matched his blood, I presume?'

Camilla followed the doctors out into the corridor where they paused to confer.

'I agree with you—probably a ruptured kidney,' Ross went on. 'He'd better have his pre-med straight away.' Writing on the notes, he glanced meaningfully at Camilla before handing them to her. 'That's Omnopon and Scopolamine, Nurse. Is anyone here with him?'

She shook her head.

'Get in touch with the next of kin then.' The registrar took himself off to alert the theatre staff.

After checking the drugs with the student, Camilla gave Mr Bolton his injection. 'This is to help you relax, and it will ease the pain a bit. Now, let's see that I've got all your details correctly. We need to tell someone where you are. Who would you like us to contact? Your wife?'

'No, I'd rather you didn't. She's visiting our son in Paris at the moment. Call my secretary . . . there's a business card in my jacket pocket.' He looked apprehensive. 'Do I gather this is serious?'

'Well, it is something that needs to be dealt with promptly,' Camilla hedged. She smiled reassuringly. 'Now don't worry, you're in excellent hands.' But she was more than a little relieved when all the preliminaries had been dealt with and it was time to pass the responsibility over to the operating team.

Back in the department, she gave the patient's business card to Ken Drew and asked if there was anything more she could do.

'We're about clear now, thanks. The pedestrian didn't make it. The others are being dealt with.' He studied the card. 'What about this guy?'

Camilla shrugged her shoulders. 'He didn't look too good. Noble said the next of kin should be told, but Mr Bolton didn't want his wife informed—she's out of the country. He said his secretary would deal with things.'

'Managing Director, Pioneer Petroleum,' Ken read. 'Seems like a big noise. Would you like to call his secretary then, since that's what he wants? You can explain the situation better than me. And he's going to Simpson afterwards, so you'll be able to follow him up.'

Having made the phone call, she returned to her own ward.

Sister Hunter had already received notice of the emergency admission. 'We've moved beds around and made room in High Dependency,' she said. 'Have a look and make sure everything's in order there, will you?'

Camilla folded the bedclothes into a theatre pack, put a transfusion stand and bed-cradle in readiness, checked oxygen and suction apparatus and placed a receiver and other equipment on the locker top.

Angus Bolton was brought to the ward at nine-thirty as she was about to go off-duty. She learned it had been necessary to remove his left kidney, but she was glad to find he had survived the operation without further complications being encountered. He was one of those patients she had spontaneously warmed to.

Relaxing after supper at the flat that night, Camilla and Marie talked about the case. Marie had been one of the theatre team.

'Ross Noble knows what he's doing . . . he did a great job,' she said.

Camilla was fitting the silver buckle on to her new navy belt. She stood up, tried it round her waist and admired the effect. 'I find him a bit starchy. What's he like in Theatre?'

'Fine. Rambled on about cricket mostly, in-between the tricky bits. Makes a nice change from Prof Purbright's fishing exploits. Perhaps I'd prefer not to get on the wrong side of him, though. He did blow his top when someone made a boo-boo.'

Neither would I, Camilla decided. But there was no reason why she should, except that you could never tell in hospital circles. When the pressure was on, tempers could get frayed. The silliest thing could spark off an atmosphere, especially when a doctor had put in a lot of work with a disappointing outcome.

Taking off the belt and rolling it up, she stretched out in her armchair and breathed a sigh of sheer bliss at the fulfilment of her years of study. 'I really thought that business with Tony would blow it for me.'

'Oh, come on,' scoffed Marie. She paused in counting the stitches on her knitting needle. 'You're much too organised to let a mere man put you off.'

Camilla smiled. 'Glad I give that impression. My mind's a ragbag really. What are you wearing to the party tomorrow night?'

They began to talk clothes, finishing up by sorting through their wardrobes before having a nightcap and going to bed.

The following morning Camilla found their emergency patient of the previous night propped up on pillows. He had already been washed by the night staff and put into hospital pyjamas. 'Good morning, Mr Bolton,' she said, coming to check that his drip was flowing correctly.

He gave a slow smile. 'Hallo, Nurse. I didn't expect to see you again. I thought you belonged in the casualty department.'

'I was just on loan to them because they were busy. How are you feeling now?' His colour had improved with the blood transfusion. 'You're looking much better.'

He laid a hand against his side. 'This wound is hell, to put it mildly.'

She made a sympathetic face. 'You've had a rough time. But we won't let you suffer . . . you'll be getting something for the pain in a minute. How about your leg? Is that comfortable?' She lifted back the covers over the bed-cradle. His fractured ankle, now in plaster, was raised on a pillow and she checked that the toes were pink.

'That's the least of my worries. May I have a drink? I'm awfully dry.'

'Just a little.' She helped him to a sip of water. 'No breakfast for you today though,' she added as the hot trolley came into the ward. 'But I don't suppose you feel like eating yet, do you?'

He shook his head. 'I shall be glad to get into my own pyjamas and have a shave. My secretary will be coming this morning . . . she's bringing the necessary. I'd like to see her. Will that be all right?'

'Yes, I'm sure it will.' She smiled and went off to see to other patients.

Hilda Brookes was still worrying them by her constant insistence on remaining an invalid, and in spite of breathing exercises with the physiotherapist she was developing a cough.

'Good morning, Hilda,' Camilla said briskly. 'Time to get up for your breakfast.'

'Oh, can't I stay here? I don't feel well.'

'I'm not surprised. Your circulation's sluggish. You must move around a bit more.' She looked at the water-jug on the locker. 'And you're hardly drinking anything. Do try to help yourself, Hilda.'

'I need a bedpan,' Mrs Brookes whined.

'We'll walk to the toilet.' Helping the unwilling patient into her dressing-gown and slippers, Camilla accompanied her to the bathroom.

Watching their slow progress, Sister Hunter shook her head in despair. Later, checking medications with Camilla, she said, 'I don't know what we're going to do about Hilda. By rights she should be going home soon but her temperature was up slightly this morning. And she eats far too many sweets. I'll have to get Noble to have a look at her, I think.'

As it happened, Jean Hunter was away for her coffee-break when the registrar came to see Mr Bolton.

Camilla tackled him about Mrs Brookes afterwards. 'Sister would like you to have a look at her. Her temperature was thirty-eight this morning. She's not a very cooperative patient.'

Mrs Brookes had been operated on before Ross Noble's return to the hospital. 'Cholecystectomy, wasn't she? May I see her notes?' he said in a businesslike fashion. Camilla handed them to him. 'She's had her "T" tube removed I see. Any problem there?'

'Not that I'm aware of. She's always had a low pain threshold though. She insists she still needs her analgesics.' Camilla followed him to the bedside and drew the curtains.

After making a careful examination of Mrs Brookes' chest, the registrar stroked his chin thoughtfully. There was a large, half-eaten slab of milk chocolate on her locker-top and there were brown traces of it on the sheet. 'You like chocolate, Mrs Brookes?' he remarked.

'Yes. Nothing wrong with that, is there?'

'It's hardly the best diet for you at the moment.'

'Well, the food here is so unappetising, I've got to eat something,' she grumbled.

His eyebrows lifted slightly, but he made no comment other than that he would arrange for her chest to be X-rayed. Back in the office he wrote out the necessary form.

'I couldn't detect much wrong with her lungs,' he said, 'but we'd better make sure. Can I have her medication sheet?'

Camilla went to get it for him and he made alterations on it. 'I'm cancelling the analgesics. Give her paracetamol if she needs anything. Is the writing legible enough for you?' he asked, handing it back.

She glanced at it. 'Fine!' she said, matching his cool tone.

Ross Noble put his pen back in his top pocket and let his shrewd eyes rove over this distracting young staff nurse, from her glowing hair to her shapely proportions. 'Anything else?' he asked, almost curtly.

'No, I don't think so. Unless,' she hesitated, 'you would like a coffee?' She knew Sister Hunter would have offered.

'No, thanks,' was his brief response and he took himself off.

His distant manner had given no indication of his thoughts.

She had the feeling of being politely put in her place. With most of the doctors she had a good relationship and it was disconcerting to be snubbed by this newcomer; it made inroads into her self-confidence. She chewed her lip with annoyance. This was the last time she would offer hospitality to Mister High and Mighty, Camilla resolved.

The evening party for the new SRNs was an informal affair. Nevertheless, the social committee had gone to some trouble to create a good atmosphere. The Doctors' Mess in the medical school was decorated with paper garlands and flashing lights, loud disco music adding to the overall gaiety.

Wearing black cords topped by a green silk shirt, Camilla felt and looked good. Marie had opted for her candy-striped silk dress which was more flattering to her fuller figure than trousers. They were a popular pair and neither lacked for company.

After bopping energetically for a while, Camilla was buttonholed by Julian. He had been indulging freely and grew increasingly soulful as he clasped her in both arms and they moved to the slow beat of an old number. Resting his forehead on hers, he gazed at her ardently.

'You know, you have the most gorgeous eyes, Ginger. They're kind of iri-iridescent . . .'

He had a little difficulty in getting out the word and Camilla giggled. 'Good thing you're not on call tonight, Julian. I wouldn't care to trust my body to your judgment.'

'Sweetheart, I'd trust my body to you anytime. How about it? My bed is but a short step . . .'

She grinned. 'Sounds like a good offer, but no thanks, I prefer my own little bed.'

His eyes widened with mock disbelief. 'What? Have I found a good girl?'

The music stopped and he dragged her over to the bar where, to Camilla's irritation, Ross Noble stood talking with Ken Drew. 'Listen, you chaps, Camilla's on the straight and narrow!' With his hand on his heart, Julian burst into loud song . . . 'The girl that I marry will have to be as soft and as sweet as Camilla C!'

Colour flooded her cheeks and she muttered, 'Shut up, Julian.'

Kenny laughed, but Ross Noble's lips twisted in a cynical smile. He said, 'If she's any sense she won't marry a doctor.'

'Why? What's wrong with doctors?' Julian demanded.

'Too many other claims on our time. Women feel slighted if they can't have one's entire attention.'

'*Women?*' Camilla gave a short laugh. 'Women are individuals. You can't bracket us all together like that, any more than you can doctors.'

His steady blue eyes held hers for what seemed like an eternity, so that in the end she had to look away. 'My experience is probably more extensive than yours,' he returned ironically. 'If marriage is your objective, I'd advise you to steer clear of the medical profession.'

'It doesn't happen to figure in my plans at present,' she said, hoping she sounded sophisticated. 'If and when it does, I shall trust my own intuition.'

'That's my girl!' Julian laid a finger against the side of his nose. 'Women's intuition . . . much better than logic. 'Scuse me a sec. Call of nature,' and he ambled off in the direction of the men's room.

Camilla had no wish to prolong the conversation. She turned to Kenny. 'Let's dance, shall we?' When they had moved out of earshot, she said, 'Ross Noble's a right ray of sunshine, isn't he? What's wrong with the man?'

He steered her past a crush of couples. 'Well, he isn't married himself, I gather. Perhaps there's a reason for his jaundiced views on the subject.'

'Mmm. He was engaged when he was here before. Perhaps it didn't work out.'

Glancing in the registrar's direction, Camilla caught his frowning gaze still upon her and quickly returned her attention to her partner.

They joined up with Marie and anaesthetist Larry Woodford for the rest of the evening, ending up in Larry's room for coffee and bedding down on his floor for the night.

But even though she joined in the light-hearted backchat, Camilla's thoughts kept straying to the peremptory registrar. Years ago her impression of him had been as an engaging personality, not the saturnine, sardonic character he now appeared to be. Yet in spite of his abrasiveness he was still subtly fascinating. She could well understand any woman getting possessive over him. Maybe his engagement had fallen apart because the girl couldn't take the demands of his profession. He had hinted as much when he had said that women felt slighted if deprived of attention.

Oh well, that was his problem. He'd boasted of having plenty of experience, so he was doubtless quite capable of sorting out his own problems.

CHAPTER THREE

ON MONDAY morning, going along to the hospital pharmacy to collect some urgent drugs, Camilla was waylaid by Julian.

'Hi, Ginger!' He put on a penitent expression. 'Look, about Saturday . . . I was tanked up, I'm afraid. Hope I didn't embarrass you?'

'Forget it,' she said lightly. 'It takes a lot to embarrass me.'

'Good! That's a load off my mind. I thought redheads had a reputation for being fiery?'

She wrinkled her pert nose at him. 'I'm fairly civilised as a rule, but don't push your luck.'

'Well, listen. There are some tickets floating around for a show at the Barbican on Thursday night. How about coming with me? They're doing *The Taming of the Shrew.*' He grinned. 'Don't take that personally.'

She considered for a moment, wondering if there was more to the invitation than an attack of conscience. Julian was a nice enough guy, but she felt nothing special for him. Not that one date amounted to anything.

But it was really the memory of Ross Noble's unsolicited advice to steer clear of the medical profession which decided her. She was not going to be influenced by *his* biased views.

'Okay. I'm on a half-day, so shall I meet you there?'

'Great! I'll walk over from the hospital and we can go back for my car afterwards. Meet you outside the entrance on the Lakeside Terrace, say seven o'clock, and we'll have cocktails first.' Looking pleased with himself, Julian carried on towards A & E while Camilla made for the pharmacy.

Arriving back on the ward, she began the morning drugs round with Avis. They reached the bay that housed both Miss Rose and Hilda Brookes. Camilla consulted their medicine charts. 'No, there's nothing for either of you this morning,' she said pleasantly.

Miss Rose, sitting by her bed reading, glanced up and smiled. In her opinion pills were anathema and she was glad to find them tailing off.

Mrs Brookes, on the other hand, looked aggrieved as she reclined on her bed. 'But I need my pain-killer,' she bleated.

Camilla checked the chart again. 'But you've been taken off those now, Hilda. Are you in pain?'

'Of course I'm in pain. I've had a serious operation, haven't I?'

'It should have eased off by now.' Camilla frowned, but remembered the timely adage . . . *pain is what the patient feels*. 'Let me have a look at your wound,' she said. Upon investigation it looked perfectly healthy. 'Well, there's no sign of inflammation and your temperature's normal now.

I'll give you some paracetamol and I'll tell Sister about it.'

Reluctantly Hilda accepted the pills, swallowed them down and took a chocolate from the box on her locker. 'Nobody cares how I suffer.'

'Of course we care,' said Camilla, 'and what about that nice husband of yours? He never misses a chance to visit you.'

'Him!' Hilda scoffed. 'He wouldn't care if I never went home. He's probably living it up with his fancy woman while I'm away.'

Recalling the careworn face of the meek little man who regularly visited his querulous wife, Camilla found that hard to believe.

As the nurses moved on to the next patient, Hilda's plaintive voice was heard asking Miss Rose if she would bring the telephone and plug it in for her. The good-natured Miss Rose obligingly went in search of it, and Avis clicked her tongue.

'She's got that dear soul on a bit of string, always getting her to fetch and carry.'

Camilla sighed in agreement. 'Nothing much we can do about it.'

The round completed and the drugs trolley safely locked away, she reported Hilda's complaint.

'Leave it with me,' said Sister Hunter. 'You get on with dressings now. Mr Bolton's drains can come out today.'

Camilla prepared her trolley and wheeled it into the single room to which Mr Bolton had been moved. It was now three days since his nephrectomy and although still weak, he was cheerful and appreciative of everything done for him. After removing the corrugated drains from his wound, she applied non-adherent dressings over the area.

'Thank you, my dear, you're most kind,' he said as she helped him back into his paisley silk pyjama jacket.

'Your drip will be coming out too, when this lot has run through,' she told him. 'Then we'll get you sitting out while we make your bed.'

'And how long do you think I'll be here, Nurse?'

'We-ell, could be a fortnight or so. There's your broken ankle to contend with as well. As soon as they put a heel on your plaster the physio will be along to teach you how to walk.'

'I suppose I must resign myself with patience.' He smoothed his dark, silvering hair and regarded her with admiration. 'At least the service is to my liking,' he said with a twinkle.

It was later in the week when catastrophe struck Simpson Ward. With Jean Hunter on days off, Camilla arrived on Wednesday to take the report. Approaching the ward, she had to step quickly out of the way as, holding an infusion bottle aloft, Night Sister sped by with an unconscious patient on a trolley. The patient was Hilda Brookes. Camilla's heart somersaulted. Her mind raced back, wondering if there was something she had failed to notice the previous day.

Eyes wide with concern, she joined the group

assembled around Matty Newbury in the office. 'What's happened to Hilda?'

Matty looked ready to burst into tears. 'She's in a coma! They've taken her to ITU. We didn't discover it until Jill was doing the TPRs this morning. She always sleeps like a log, hardly ever drinks her morning tea. We didn't dream . . .'

'What was it, an MI?'

'Wish it was.' Matty chewed her lip. 'They say she's taken an overdose.'

Camilla's mouth dropped open. 'Oh no! But how could she?'

Matty spread her hands despairingly. 'We gave her nothing but paracetamol. The drugs trolley was never left unlocked, and I always keep the keys to the drugs cupboard in my pocket.' She fished them out to show Camilla.

The whole of the day staff stood around with long faces. There was going to be trouble.

'Well, we'd best get on with the report before they start the inquisition,' sighed Camilla.

The report had just been completed when Night Sister returned, her expression grim. 'Now, Nurse Newbury and Nurse Clifton, I want every drug checked against the records. The rest of you can get on with your work.'

With the two staff nurses she went through every tablet and ampoule and mixture in the ward stocks. Every item was accounted for.

Night Sister scratched her head and admitted herself baffled. 'All right, Nurse Newbury,' she said, not unkindly, 'you'd better get off to your bed. Everything seems to be in order here, but there'll have to be an enquiry. Let's hope the woman recovers so that we can get to the bottom of this.'

The day staff went about their duties with heavy hearts. Patients within sight of Hilda's bed were equally downcast and Miss Rose was quite tearful. 'Oh, that poor woman,' she said. 'I wish I'd been kinder to her.'

'Miss Rose, nobody could have been kinder to her than you,' Camilla said.

'What was it? A heart attack?'

'We don't know yet what it was,' returned Camilla tactfully.

Hilda's vacant bed was stripped, disinfected and made up with clean linen. Her belongings were gathered together in a plastic bag and taken for safe keeping until required.

It was midday when Ross Noble strode into the office where Camilla was sorting forms. She looked up to see him glowering at her. 'Mrs Brookes,' he announced in an ominously quiet voice, 'is dead.'

Her heart lurched. 'Oh! Oh dear. I *am* sorry.'

His blue eyes were like steel as he banged a fist on the filing cabinet. 'That woman should *never* have died! She'd made a perfectly good recovery from surgery. There was nothing wrong with her. Where the hell did she get Distalgesics from?'

'Distalgesics? Was that what it was?' Camilla frowned and shook her head in bewilderment. 'It beats me. I'd been wondering whether she'd been secretly collecting those strong pain-killers you took her off.'

'Give me strength!' he exploded. 'What goes on in this ward, girl? Don't you make *sure* people take their medication?'

'Yes, of course.' She managed to keep the heat out of her voice. 'Short of inspecting their mouths after they've taken a drink, there's nothing more we can do.' His attitude infuriated her, but she could hardly afford to show it until it was found where the blame lay.

He shot her an accusing glance from under his straight brows. 'And there's no way she could have got at your stocks?'

'No. As far as I'm aware, the drugs trolley is always locked unless someone's with it.'

'I hope, for all your sakes, that's true. She got them from somewhere. You *did* search her property, I assume,' he added satirically.

She nodded. 'There was half a tube of indigestion tablets in her handbag, that's all.'

'All right . . . I'll check on my other patients now,' he growled.

On the ward round he was polite, as usual, to the patients. No one would have guessed that he had just ripped Camilla to pieces; unless they noticed that he virtually ignored her except when issuing instructions. She knew that underneath he was a simmering volcano. It was as though his anger at Hilda's death was directed entirely at her. The injustice of it made her seethe. *Drop dead!* she thought rebelliously.

Later in the afternoon Hilda's forlorn little husband arrived to collect her belongings.

'Mr Brookes, we're all so very sorry,' Camilla began.

His face contorted and he started to weep. Great silent tears trickled down his lined cheeks. Camilla put her arm around him and led him to a chair. 'I know, it must have been an awful shock to you. It was a shock to us all.'

He fumbled in his pocket for a handkerchief and blew his nose. 'Y-you know, I loved that girl. Sh-she was always accusing me of having someone else, someone at the office,' he confided. 'But I never did . . . it was all her imagination . . .'

Camilla sat with him and let him unburden himself, trying to find the right things to say to ease his distress. When he was calmer she made him some tea and went to fetch his wife's possessions for him to check and sign for.

She was about to return with the things when Avis came hurrying towards her.

'Camilla! Look!' Avis handed her a small brown bottle with one tablet in it. 'Miss Rose dropped some money and some of it rolled under Hilda's locker. When I moved it out to get it for her, I found this.'

Camilla read the chemist's label. *Mrs H Brookes. Distalgesic. Two to be taken as directed.*

The two nurses looked at each other. 'Thanks,

Avis,' Camilla said. 'I'll see if her husband knows anything about them.'

A guilty flush suffused Mr Brookes' face when she showed him the bottle and questioned him. 'Oh, those. Y-yes,' he gulped. 'They're some she had at home, from the doctor. Sh-she made me bring them in the other night . . . said yours weren't any good.'

'How many were there in the bottle, do you remember?'

'We-ell, more than half full I reckon, Nurse. I—I wondered if it was all right. Only if I didn't do what she wanted . . . sh-she wouldn't speak to me.' He began to weep again.

Camilla's feelings alternated with profound relief at having discovered the answer to the tragedy and compassion for the misguided Mr Brookes. 'Oh dear. That wasn't very sensible,' she said gently. 'You should have told us. Look, if you wouldn't mind hanging on for a few moments, I think the doctor would like to speak to you.'

She asked the switchboard to bleep Ross Noble and when he answered she reported what had been found.

There was a slight pause before he said, 'I see. Keep him there. I'll be along.'

Arriving on the ward some ten minutes later, he had a private talk with the grieving Mr Brookes. They left together, Ross's arm resting consolingly around the man's bowed shoulders.

Whether Hilda had taken too many pills by

accident or design to spite her husband would never be known for certain, but for the staff of Simpson Ward it was an enormous relief to find that no one there had been guilty of neglect. Nevertheless, they were all sad about Hilda. She had always been her own worst enemy.

Thinking about the night staff, Camilla said, 'Can we get a message to Matty somehow? She must still be worried sick.'

'I'll slip a message under her door when I go off if she's not awake,' promised Avis. 'She lives above me in the nurses' home.'

'I certainly won't forget my first week as a staff nurse,' Camilla told Marie later that night.

'So *that's* what's been wrong with Noble today. We could hardly get a civil word out of him. Oh well, all water under the bridge.'

'And he never even came back to say sorry, the rat.' Camilla scowled. 'Beneath his dignity, I suppose. Bet he wouldn't have spoken to Sister Hunter like that if she'd been on duty. I shall give him the big frost from now on.'

Marie was a placid girl who was content to let troubles take care of themselves. Her own life ran on smooth lines. She had Luke, her steady boy-friend, who worked in a City bank and adored her, and she was on good terms with everyone.

'Forget it,' she advised. 'It'll all blow over. Not worth upsetting yourself.'

'I suppose not. Anyway,' Camilla said more

cheerfully, 'I've got something nice to look forward to tomorrow. Julian's taking me to see some Shakespeare at the Barbican.'

Marie raised her eyebrows. 'You're living dangerously. You know his reputation.'

'Listen, I wouldn't have survived at St Martin's for three years without knowing how to take care of myself. I've dealt with doctors like Julian before . . . and patients. And it's mostly hot air.'

Getting ready the following evening, Camilla decided she had better wear something decent for the occasion. It was pleasantly warm and she settled for a silky dress, boldly striped in vivid blues and greens, taking a throw-over scarf to put round her shoulders if it should turn chilly later.

Alighting at the Barbican station, she walked the short distance to the Centre and made her down the flight of steps leading to the Waterside Terrace. It was a pleasant rendezvous for the City's workers, a floodlit oasis amid the surrounding high-rise buildings. A few ducks bobbed lazily on the water and people took their ease at the small tables dotted about on the terrace outside the refreshment rooms.

As arranged, Julian was waiting for her at the entrance to the Centre. He greeted her with a friendly kiss and put an arm round her waist as they strolled through into the carpeted reception area. It was milling with people going in various directions.

'I don't know whether the others are here yet,'

Julian said, leading her towards one of the bars.

'What others?' Camilla asked.

'There were four tickets going, courtesy of one of the livery companies. I believe Ross Noble had the others . . . Oh, there they are! Let's join them.'

Camilla's heart sank as she spotted the tall figure of the registrar among the crowd. His fair hair gleamed under the lights and his elegant fawn suit sat easily on his large frame.

Damn! she thought as Julian propelled her in that direction. What had promised to be an enjoyable evening now took on a different outlook. She could have wished herself anywhere but there.

It took her a moment to recognise Ross's companion. It was Sister Hunter, looking totally different out of uniform, her attractive dark hair loose and flowing.

'Hallo, Sister.' Camilla greeted her with a glad smile. 'How nice to see you.' She ignored the registrar.

'Oh, do call me Jean,' said Sister Hunter. 'Ross decided my education needed improving,' she added drily. 'I'm not really into Shakespeare, but this one's not too heavy, is it?'

'What can I get you to drink?' Ross asked.

Camilla gave him a wintry smile and said she would like a dry Martini.

'I hear you've been having a big drama on the ward,' Jean said as the men stood at the bar waiting to be served.

'Don't remind me!' Camilla gave a huge sigh.

'Was I relieved when we found that bottle.'

Jean smiled in sympathy. 'I bet you were. I was lucky to miss out on that one.'

Returning with their drinks, Ross caught the drift of their conversation. 'Yes, it was quite hairy for a while. Wasn't it, Camilla?' He looked at her pointedly, his lips twitching.

'For us it was. And you didn't even have the grace to apologise for yelling at me.'

'Apologise for expecting efficiency? Come on, a hospital is only as good as its personnel. We have to keep you on your toes. Can't risk losing our reputation.'

He looked so superior she could have hit him. With her chin in the air, she retorted, 'There were no complaints on our ward until you arrived.'

'Anyone for an olive branch?' ventured Julian, handing round a dish of crisps.

It was time to find their way to the theatre. Their seats were in pairs, one couple behind the other. Camilla was glad not to be sitting alongside Ross, but she would have preferred him to be in front of them and not vice versa. She would have liked to be able to observe him undetected rather than the other way around. Not that he probably even remembered her existence now that they were apart, she mused.

Julian pulled her arm companionably through his and they studied the programme together. She settled down to enjoy the evening, trying to put the exasperating registrar out of her mind. But his uproarious laughter as the comedy unfolded made that virtually impossible. So apparently he did still have a sense of humour, even though he kept it well hidden where she was concerned.

The performance was excellent and at the end of the evening they left the auditorium in cheerful mood, discussing the players.

'I think old Will had a point there. It's about time you girls showed us more respect,' Julian said.

Camilla grinned and dug him in the ribs with her forefinger. 'This is the twentieth century, not the sixteenth, mate.'

'Much as I agree with the Bard's sentiments,' put in Ross serenely, 'I don't agree with starving them into submission. Shall we feed them, Julian?'

'Great . . . so long as they'll settle for a Wimpy.' Julian pulled out an empty pocket lining.

Ross glanced at his watch. 'It's too late for eating out around here anyway. Will you settle for raiding my freezer?'

'Super,' Jean agreed. 'We'll see if you operate in the kitchen as well as you do in Theatre.'

'Self-preservation.' Ross gave a twisted smile. 'I should have wasted away if I'd waited for anyone else to cook for me. We can walk to my flat from here.' He led the way.

Nobody had consulted Camilla about what she wanted to do. Julian held her hand and she had no option but to go along with him. Not that she really minded. The comedy had put her in a better frame of mind. In fact she was quite curious to see where

Ross Noble lived. Homes could often be revealing about their owners.

It was a very classy fourth floor flat. The living-room had a big picture window leading on to a balcony which looked out over the lake. Furnished with chrome and leather furniture on a russet carpet, the room was typically masculine. There was a large desk on which were folders, filing trays, telephone and an angle poise lamp, while a fitment with stacked stereo, drinks bar and bookshelves occupied the whole of one wall.

'Make yourselves at home.' Ross flung his jacket on to a chair and removed his tie.

'Anything we can do?' asked Jean.

'No. I don't allow women to mess around in my kitchen. Julian can be my dogsbody. Amuse yourselves for ten minutes, girls.' He waved his hands airily. 'You'll find tapes over there.'

Jean searched among his collection, found a Simon and Garfunkel cassette and popped it into the stereo. She smiled. 'This takes me back to when Duncan and I first met.'

Camilla discovered that Jean had a fiancé in the merchant navy. He was due home soon after a long voyage. They talked about him and his travels and Jean confided that he was hoping for a shore-based job with his shipping company so that they could buy a house somewhere and settle down.

In between times Camilla gazed around her, soaking up the atmosphere of the room. She noticed a framed photograph of an elderly couple in a niche by the bookshelves and went up to look at it. The couple were in full evening dress, obviously attending some official function. The woman had a kindly smile and the man the same distinguished bearing as Ross. She assumed they might be his parents.

Browsing through the bookshelves, she saw among weighty medical tomes, profiles of prominent cricketers and rugby players.

Sounds of activity came from the kitchen; a clinking of crockery, a burst of song from Julian and a sudden laugh from Ross. A pleasantly appetising aroma began to steal on the air and in a relatively short space of time Ross called, 'Come and get it!'

'Smells good,' Jean enthused as the two girls ventured into the hallowed precincts of the kitchen. It was well equipped with pine-laminated cupboards and work surfaces and a breakfast bar and stools along one wall.

Ross brought a succulent-looking concoction from the oven. '*Voila!* Moussaka suit everyone? Grab a plate and help yourselves.'

Julian was hacking chunks off a crusty loaf and piling them in a basket. 'He's a clever lad, isn't he?'

'Certainly handy to have around the house,' said Jean.

Camilla dug her spoon into the savoury mixture. 'How did you do it so quickly?'

Uncorking a bottle of red wine, Ross poured

four glasses. 'Here's to me! And my favourite delicatessen,' he added.

'You old fraud!' exclaimed Jean amid general laughter.

Her earlier misgivings now gone, Camilla found herself relaxing and really enjoying the impromptu get together. She even found herself warming to the maddening registrar, although there was still something about him that repelled familiarity. Watching him covertly as they sat over coffee in the living-room afterwards, she glimpsed odd flashes of the old Ross through that armour-plated reserve.

Julian raised the subject of the June Field Day which was held annually at the hospital sports ground. This year St Martin's were challenging the Great Central to a cricket match. 'You going to turn out for us, Ross? You were a Cambridge blue, weren't you?'

'Well, yes. But I'm out of practice. They're not strong on cricket in the States.'

'Oh, you'll soon get back into form with a bit of work in the nets. Can't let the GCH put one over on us.'

Jean patted a yawn. 'Before you two get bogged down with cricket, it's time I went home. I'm on an early tomorrow.'

'That goes for me too, I suppose,' said Julian, stretching. 'You'll have to walk back to the hospital with me to collect my car, Ginger.'

'Where do you live?' Ross enquired with a casual glance at her.

'Islington,' she said.

'That's in my direction,' Jean remarked.

'Fine, I can drop Julian off at the hospital first and then deliver both of you.'

The suggestion took Julian by surprise and he looked slightly disconcerted. 'Oh, there's no need to trouble you . . .'

'No trouble at all,' declared Ross. There was an air of authority about the man that silenced argument.

They all made for the underground park where his gleaming white Jaguar stood waiting.

Camilla climbed into the back with Julian. She sensed his disappointment. He'd probably had in mind a very different end to the evening. 'Thanks for asking me,' she said, turning to him with a warm smile. 'I've had a lovely time, Julian.'

He took her chin in his hands and planted a discreet but lingering kiss on her lips. 'We'll do it again sometime soon, eh, Ginge?'

Within five minutes he was alighting and making his lone way to the residents' quarters at the hospital. Ross drove on towards Islington, following Camilla's directions. Depositing her at her flat, he drove off promptly again with Jean.

But that curious, self-satisfied smile twisting his lips did not escape her. She felt an odd sense of pique as she let herself into the house. His triumphant expression suggested he had achieved his objective; to thwart Julian's attempt to prolong his evening with her. Not that she had wished to do so, but it was her decision to make and no business of Ross Noble's. She resented his interference in her affairs. What right had he to order her comings and goings?

CHAPTER FOUR

WITH THE next two days off, Camilla decided that perhaps it was about time she showed her face at home. She thought she would go down and surprise them. Packing her weekend case, she stowed it on the back seat of her Mini and left about nine a.m. on Friday morning for the long haul to Christchurch.

Her mind busy with the events of the past few days, the miles sped by. She relived the business with Mrs Brookes and Ross Noble's hostile attitude about the overdose. That man was intolerable. Unless, of course, she had over-reacted as she was sometimes inclined to do. She had felt pretty scared about the incident until the source of the pills had come to light. They all had. Maybe his backlash was understandable, but he should have apologised for sounding off the way he did.

Strangely enough, last night at his flat after their theatre trip, she had *almost* liked him. He could be utterly charming when he chose, although she'd seen precious little of that side of his character so far.

By midday she had reached the pleasant country town of Lyndhurst where she stopped to buy flowers for her mother. She chose some blue irises and pink pyrethrums which looked really lovely together.

Then on through the green and lush landscape, passing New Forest ponies grazing on the heathland, and banks of golden gorse and purple heather. Cottage gardens were tipsy with lilac and laburnum. The peace of the rural scene was in sharp contrast to the feverish pace of London, and already she began to feel refreshed.

Towards the coast, stately pines were silhouetted against the skyline. Another hour brought Camilla to her home town just beyond Christchurch and soon her tyres were crunching to a halt outside the old vicarage. There were signs of activity in the large grounds. A marquee had been erected on the side lawn and trestle tables waited to be filled with produce. She had quite forgotten about the annual Spring Garden Fête.

Gathering her flowers in her hand, she rang the front doorbell. It was answered by her mother's daily help.

'Hallo, Edith,' Camilla said brightly.

Edith's mouth dropped open. 'Hallo, lovey. I didn't know you was coming?'

'Neither did I until last night. Anyone in?'

'Yes, they're in the kitchen having a snack lunch. Your ma's been telling us how you passed your exams 'n that. They're real proud of you, dear.'

'Well, I'm quite chuffed about it myself,' grinned Camilla. She went through to the large family kitchen with her flowers. 'Surprise! Surprise!'

'Camilla!' her mother exclaimed. 'Oh dear. I wish you'd let us know. Your bedroom's full of stuff for the white elephant stall. How long have you got?'

Camilla knew it wasn't meant to sound unwelcoming. It was just that her mother planned her days with precision and the unexpected was inclined to put her out.

'Only until tomorrow, Mummy . . . I shall have to go back in the evening as I'm working on Sunday. I just felt like seeing you all.' She went round to kiss everyone.

Her father boomed, 'Well, you couldn't have come at a better time. We shall need all the help we can get tomorrow.'

'I suppose you've had no lunch.' Mrs Clifton got up and went over to the stove. 'There's some soup left here if you'd like it, and I'll make some more toast.'

'Yes, come and sit down, darling, and tell us all your news,' put in her grandmother. 'You look blooming.' She cast an approving glance at her granddaughter's clear, creamy complexion and burnished hair. 'Any new young man on the horizon?'

'No . . . no one in particular. But life's quite hectic enough without that.'

'You could do worse than think about young Stephen,' suggested her father. 'He's got a soft spot for you, I know.'

Young Stephen, the curate, was a man of thirty,

an eager-beaver full of ideas on updating religion and pulling in the young people.

Camilla laughed and got on with her soup. 'I didn't come down to find a husband, Dad.'

They chatted on for a while before her mother said, 'You'll have to excuse me, Camilla . . . I must get on. I've promised to do some baking for the refreshments. But you take your time. I'll get Edith to clear that stuff out of your room presently.'

The Reverend Clifton also disappeared into his study to prepare his Sunday sermon, leaving Camilla with her grandmother. But that was nothing new. It was usually like that, family life having to be fitted in around the needs of the parish, and she accepted it philosophically.

As always, the vicarage seemed to be the focal point of half the local population. People drifted in and out on various missions and the telephone rang constantly.

Camilla entered into the spirit of things, making herself agreeable to folks she had come to know over the years, lending a hand with receiving and sorting out offerings for the fête. Having changed into white cotton trousers and a blue sleeveless top, she sat cross-legged on the floor of the living-room sorting through piles of books.

'Well, this is an unexpected pleasure!' Stephen Evans dropped to the floor beside her, his brown spaniel eyes showing frank delight. Stephen was as lean as a bean-pole with a mop of dark curly hair and he had grown a full beard since her last visit at

Christmas. 'I was thinking of coming to look you up—we've got a revivalist meeting in London shortly. But I suppose you're a busy girl?'

He plied her with questions about her life at the hospital, wanting to know if she would be making a change on having finished her training. 'There are good hospitals in this part of the world, you know. Wouldn't you like to be nearer home . . . to swop the noisy city for our smashing small corner?'

'Mmm . . .' she pondered. 'It has its attractions, but I like being where the action is.'

'Plenty of action here too, if you look for it. We're having square dancing in the parish hall after the fête tomorrow . . . Will you be able to come?'

'Oh, I don't think so, Steve. It takes me about four hours to drive back so I want to leave around eight at the latest.'

'Not just for an hour?' he coaxed.

'Well, I won't promise.'

She was rather relieved when he was called away to supervise erection of some of the side-stalls.

The rest of the day passed in a whirl of activity. It was midnight before Camilla tumbled into bed after picking her way around the overflow of goods on the landing. Even then she lay sleepless for some time. Stephen's arguments were thought-provoking. She was not unaware of the personal incentive behind them and she tried to weigh up the pros and cons of her life.

Ought she to settle for the comfortable existence of a country parish? It could be as demanding or undemanding as you liked to make it. Here was security and permanence. On the other hand, there was a kind of excitement about her work in the large London hospital. It appealed to her far more than taking Sunday School classes or doing the host of other things that clergy wives got involved in. She was not really a groupie. She liked one-to-one relationships. And besides that, although she admired Stephen, he did not remotely arouse her.

There was no chemistry, no tingle down her spine when he looked at her. In fact the arrogant Ross Noble could cause more turbulence in her innards with one of his powerful, calculating looks. She didn't know why she should suddenly have thought of him again, but subconsciously she felt a strange reluctance to move out of his orbit.

She was determined to break through that ivory tower he had built for himself. It represented a kind of challenge. She would make him accept her on equal terms. After that he could go to hell.

Saturday morning dawned bright and beautiful. By the time Camilla was bathed and dressed, the vicarage and grounds were astir with activity as final preparations for the afternoon got underway.

It fell to her lot to run the children's races with Stephen. She also sold raffle tickets, dried the tears of lost toddlers and put a plaster on a grazed knee. She helped with the teas.

At five o'clock stall-holders began to pack up and the crowd to disperse. Camilla drifted back to the house to put her things together. Edith prepared high tea for the family and Stephen joined them for a meal of cold meats and salad. There was great satisfaction around the dining-table as they discussed the success of the afternoon, proceeds of which were to go to the building of an extension to the church hall.

'So will you come to the dance tonight?' Stephen asked Camilla.

'No, I'd better not, thanks all the same. I want to get back before midnight . . . I've been burning the candle lately.' Actually the novelty of the country weekend had begun to pall and she was itching to get back to her own life.

'Mummy,' Camilla went on, 'do you mind if I pick some primroses? I'd like to take some back for my flatmate and Sister Hunter.' There were masses of the pale, starry clumps on the banks of the brook at the far end of the garden.

'By all means, help yourself,' her mother said. 'You don't need to ask.'

'Excuse me then. I'll do that now.'

In the shed she unearthed an old strawberry punnet and lined it with damp kitchen-roll. Then she ran down through the tall grasses to the brook and enjoyed herself gathering the sweet-smelling blooms and pale green leaves.

Stephen had wandered down after her. He sat on the ancient garden-seat by the bank, watching her closely.

'I'm sorry you're going,' he said as she finished picking and stood up.

'Yes. It's been a lovely break.'

He patted the seat beside him. 'Sit and talk for a minute. I really did mean that about looking you up when I came to town.'

'Yes, do,' she said brightly.

'You know, you're far too attractive for any bloke's peace of mind.'

She saw the warmth in his brown eyes and buried her nose in her flowers. 'Curates aren't supposed to say things like that.'

'Why not? I haven't taken a vow of celibacy.' He paused. 'You know what I'm driving at, don't you? Camilla, I'm very fond of you . . .'

She stopped him quickly before he could go any further. 'Please, Steve, don't. Just because I'm a vicar's daughter doesn't make me the right kind of person for you. I'd make the most awful partner for a parish priest. I'm not in the least committee-minded . . . and I couldn't cut myself up into little pieces like my mother does.'

'But you do that already, in your work, don't you?'

She shook her head. 'It's not the same. Besides . . .'

'Besides . . . you mean . . . I don't turn you on,' he finished for her.

She put a hand on his. 'Don't be offended . . . I'm fond of you too, but as a friend.'

'Oh! So may I still come and see you when I'm in town? Faint heart ne'er won fair lady.'

Camilla laughed. 'Nobody could accuse you of

being a faintheart. Come on, I have to go.'

They returned to the house in companionable silence.

'You still won't change your mind about the dance?' he persisted. She shook her head. 'Okay. Bye, then. Safe journey. I'll be in touch.'

It was dusk by the time Camilla left Christchurch. The family waved her off with a dutiful show of affection and said she shouldn't leave it so long next time. She knew they had been glad to see her but that they wouldn't pine at her departure. And perhaps she was lucky to have independent parents. Some of her friends' families could be overpowering in their demands for attention. On the whole, Camilla was glad she was allowed to lead a life of her own.

Marie and Luke were having coffee together when Camilla arrived back at midnight. Marie went into raptures over the primroses. 'Oh, aren't they gorgeous,' she said.

There were empty glasses and a champagne bottle on the coffee table. Camilla also noticed that the pair of them seemed even more dreamy-eyed than usual. 'What have you two been celebrating?'

'Luke's got his promotion,' said Marie, sighing ecstatically.

'Oh, great! Tell me about it then!'

'Assistant manager at a local branch of my bank near Tonbridge,' said Luke with a modest smile.

'Which means that we can make positive plans to get married,' added Marie.

'That's terrific. Oh!' Camilla looked suddenly woebegone. 'That means I'll be having to look for a new flatmate.'

'Not for a month or two. He doesn't start there till July, and there's a lot to arrange first. Anyway, you won't have any problems. There's always someone wanting to share a flat.'

After fixing herself a coffee, Camilla diplomatically went off to bed, leaving the other two still mulling over their future plans.

'You'll never guess who we've got in the other side ward,' said Jean Hunter when Camilla reported for duty at midday on Sunday.

'Who's that?'

'Fern Debden.'

'Who's Fern Debden? Oh! You mean . . . the girl who played Kate in *The Taming of the Shrew*!'

'Yes. She was admitted on Friday with appendicitis. Her room is like a florist's shop and there's been a constant stream of visitors. Julian saw her in A & E . . . he keeps finding excuses to pop in and see her again.

Camilla chuckled. 'That figures. She's doing okay then?'

'Yes. A bit sorry for herself. She's still got a drain in, but she'll be fine. The only other new patient is Amy Whipple, forty. Bit of a sad character. Living at the YWCA. She's in for investigation.

Chest pains and stomach cramps. The number of operations she's had, poor woman, it might be adhesions. Her temperature's erratic. Ross is puzzled. He wants to run some more tests before he decides what to do. Meantime he's put her on antibiotics. Well,' Jean beamed, 'I'm off to Tilbury now.'

'Oh, your fiancé's ship is in, is it?'

'Yes, he's got a week's leave, so I'm taking some of mine. The off-duty's all written up, so everything should be plain sailing for you. Thanks for the primroses, but I'll leave them here as we're going away.'

'Okay, have a good time,' Camilla said. She arranged the flowers in a bowl and put them on the desk.

Sunday was normally a leisurely day with no rounds. Visitors would occupy patients' attention for most of the afternoon, but there were still the essentials to be done before the influx.

Two of the staff set about getting patients back to bed, attending to toilet needs and pressure areas. Another got on with the four-hourlies and Camilla co-opted Sally, a pupil nurse new to the ward, to help her with the drugs round.

They started with Mr Bolton who was sitting out in his chair, now well on the road to recovery. He gave Camilla a welcoming smile.

'It's good to see you back, my dear. Did you have nice days off?'

'Lovely, thanks. I went home. You've had your

stitches out, I hear, and you've got a heel on your plaster now. How's it going?'

'With difficulty . . . but I'm persevering,' he said cheerfully. 'The wound is still rather tender, but I hope to be going home fairly soon.'

'Well, let's get you back to bed before your visitors arrive.' They plumped his pillows and made him comfortable before giving his medication.

Their next call was to the adjacent side ward where Fern Debden wilted. She looked even more delectable off stage than on, with her long auburn hair riotous about her bare shoulders. Her ivory sheer silk nightie had the thinnest of ribbon straps. Her touching vulnerability would have melted the hardest heart, Camilla thought.

'I saw your last performance at the Barbican,' she said after introducing herself. 'It was great.'

'You too?' Fern's voice was husky and languorous. 'Half the hospital seems to have been there.'

Camilla laughed. 'Just four of us, as far as I know. It so happened we're all connected with this ward. How are you feeling?' She poured the actress a drink and gave her the prescribed tablets.

'Ghastly,' sighed Fern.

'You'll be surprised what a difference a couple of days will make. What lovely flowers.' Camilla looked around at the display.

'Look, if you want any for the ward, do take some.' Fern waved a limp hand. 'It's stupid having all these in here.'

'All right, I'll see if there's anyone without.'

Carrying on with the medicines, they presently came to the other new patient, Amy Whipple. In contrast to the glamorous actress, she looked a pathetic sight in her hospital nightdress. Short, poker-straight mousy hair framed her plump cheeks which were blotchy with broken veins.

'Hallo, Miss Whipple,' Camilla smiled at her as she handed over the antibiotics. 'I hear you're something of a mystery at the moment.'

Amy Whipple nodded. 'Yes, the doctors don't know what to make of me. And my notes seem to have gone missing 'n all. They want to do more tests . . . Wish they'd make up their minds. I think it's something to do with me liver. This pain keeps gripping me.'

Camilla looked sympathetic. 'Well, they have to be certain before they know how to act. Are you expecting some visitors today?'

'No, ducks. I don't know anyone in London. I just came down from York last week. Lost my job up there so thought I'd given this place a try. Seems like my luck was out, don't it?'

Camilla and Sally exchanged compassionate glances as they carried on. Miss Whipple did seem to be one of life's unfortunates.

The work finished, the ward was opened to visitors. They trickled in with eager faces, bearing gifts and bunches of flowers. Remembering Fern Debden's offer, Camilla thought she would take her at her word and scrounge some of the surplus flowers for Amy.

Fern was holding court with four visitors, all from the cast of the play. One of the men sat stroking her hand, gazing at her ardently. At Camilla's appearance he looked up and said, 'Oh, Nurse darling, have you come to chuck some of us out?'

She grinned. 'Let's say I'm not seeing too well this afternoon. Actually, Miss Debden, there is a lady in the ward who'd appreciate some flowers if you've any to spare.'

'Yes, of course. Take the carnations—and will you put these in water?' said Fern languidly.

'Sure.' Camilla gathered up the bouquet of long-stemmed pink roses from the bed and left to arrange them. Returning, she put them on the bed-table, exchanging them for the vase of carnations. Outside in the corridor she collided with Julian. 'Hallo, what do you want?'

'Nothing special,' he grinned. 'We're quiet downstairs, so thought I'd pop in and see our celebrity.'

'Well, I don't think you'd get in at the moment. She's got four visitors in there already.'

'Oh well,' he said cheerfully, 'I'll have to settle for a cup of tea with you, Ginger. Anyway, we didn't finish our tête-á-tête properly the other night, did we?' His bleep sounding just then made him groan. 'So that's that. Bye for now then. I'll be in touch.'

'I'll tell the lady you were enquiring,' Camilla

called after him with good-natured irony.

She took the carnations along to Miss Whipple. 'A lady in the side ward sent these to you. She's got lots.'

The woman brightened. 'That's nice of her. Funny how some people gets everything and others get nothing.'

'The luck of the draw, Amy,' said Camilla.

Afternoon teas had arrived and she took a tray in to Mr Bolton. His wife and son were seated with him and he introduced them both. The son, Dominic, was a slighter version of his father, but equally polished and debonair. He eyed Camilla with a one-sided smile.

'Really, Father, I'm amazed at your impatience to leave this place if this is the quality of the staff.'

Camilla was used to fielding gratuitous compliments from smooth young men. 'Everyone's impatient to leave us,' she sighed. 'It's demoralising really.'

'We've been wondering what we can do to show our appreciation,' put in Mrs Bolton. 'Do you think a barbecue would be popular? We usually have one in the summer at our place on the river at Maidenhead.'

'That sounds lovely,' Camilla said.

'All right, as soon as I'm mobile we'll see what we can arrange.' Mr Bolton tapped his plastered leg. 'How long do I have to carry this thing around?'

'Usually about three months, but you'll get quite used to walking with it.' She smiled and left them to their family party.

The rest of the day passed uneventfully and travelling home on the Underground that night, Camilla was well content with her lot. She felt that she had come to the right decision where Stephen was concerned.

The following afternoon Professor Purbright made his tour of the ward with Ross and little Dr Lucy. Mr Bolton was progressing satisfactorily and Miss Rose got her marching orders, much to her delight.

The doctors spent a fair time with Amy Whipple. Professor Purbright was his usual vague, kindly, unforthcoming self. Camilla thought that Ross's attitude was rather taciturn, but his fluctuating moods no longer surprised her.

'I was ever so sick this morning,' Miss Whipple told them.

'Really?' said Ross. 'Did you show a nurse?'

'Oh no . . . I was in the loo. I just pulled the handle.'

'If it happens again, please call someone. We'd like to see it,' he said.

Moving on, the doctors had a long private discussion as they left the ward.

Later that day Ross returned to write up case notes, X-ray forms and requests for blood tests. Camilla found him folders and listened to instructions. She asked if anything had been decided about Miss Whipple and he replied that they were still investigating.

Finishing his writing, he clipped his pen in his top pocket, leaned back in the chair and fixed her with an appraising stare. 'You've been missing for the past couple of days.'

'Yes. I went home.'

'Where's home?'

'In Dorset . . . near Christchurch.'

'Thomas Hardy country. I've never been there.' He nodded at the primroses. 'Was that where they came from?'

'Yes. It's especially beautiful at this time of year.'

'You left your scarf at my flat the other night,' he said.

'Did I? I hadn't missed it.'

'I keep forgetting to bring it in. Would it be out of your way to call for it when you go off tonight?'

'No . . . I can go that way.'

He nodded. 'Okay . . . I'll be there. I'll expect you.'

It was nine-thirty before she got off. She was quite tired. It had been overcast all day and now the rain had begun in earnest. Although she was wearing a lightweight jacket, Camilla had no umbrella and she regretted having promised to call for the scarf. Having said that she would, however, she felt Ross might be annoyed if she didn't. Especially if he had stayed in because of it. She ran most of the way and arrived wet and breathless.

When he answered the door to her ring he said

airily, 'Oh! I'd forgotten you were coming.'

So I needn't have bothered, she thought, with a shade of annoyance.

Casually dressed in brown cords and a fawn sweat shirt, he looked superbly manly. 'You'd better come in and dry off.'

'Thank you.' She gave her wet hair a shake.

'Give me your jacket and go and towel yourself in the bathroom.'

She left him shaking the jacket and did as he said. After drying her face on a soft brown towel, she rubbed at her hair, put a comb through it and emerged pink-cheeked and glowing, if still a little damp.

Ross had made her a coffee and set it on the low table on which also lay her scarf, neatly folded. 'Sit down.' He flopped into a chair himself, propping one muscular leg across the other knee.

She felt oddly ill at ease and completely lacking in poise, sitting alone with him in his living-room. It had been different with the others there. It did not occur to her that her eyes were luminous and that she looked infinitely desirable.

His magnetic gaze travelled over her and her heart began to skitter nervously. To fill the uncomfortable silence, she said, 'Funny that Fern Debden should land up on Simpson Ward. She's even prettier close up, isn't she?'

'I gather you're not the only one who thinks so.' Ross gave a derisive smile. 'Julian Gilmore seems to be of the same opinion by all accounts.'

She sipped her coffee. 'Oh, does he?'

Suddenly he rapped out, 'So you decided to ignore my advice to steer clear of doctors?'

The remark shook Camilla. She gave a light laugh. 'What brought that on? Because I went to the theatre with Julian? Surely who I go with is my concern?'

'Well, don't say you weren't warned.'

Camilla was incensed at his presumption. 'Look,' she flared, 'why don't you mind your own business? I don't know what kind of a bad experience you've had, but it's no good going around with a chip on your shoulder . . .'

His jaw jutted ominously. 'Don't you lecture me, young woman.'

Camilla tossed her head. She set down her mug and stood up, her insides churning. 'Oh, put your chin away, you look ridiculous.'

The blue eyes flashed fire. 'And you should learn just how far you can go . . . standing there with every inch of you asking to be seduced.'

Her own eyes widened. 'I can't help the workings of your low mind,' she snapped.

He too had risen. With his hands in his pockets he stood there, studying her indolently, his lip curling. 'Don't tell me you're not aware of your own physical attractions.'

'Oh, go and jump in the lake. I'm not prepared to walk around in a nun's habit with my eyes cast down to save *your* animal instincts getting out of control.'

'My animal instincts are perfectly under control.'

'*Are* they?' Her tone dared him to prove it.

His lips tightened into a stern line. Her heart began to thump painfully as, purposefully, he came towards her. Then, taking her by the shoulders, his mouth came down over hers. Every bone in her body seemed to be liquifying as the pressure of his lips increased. She was powerless to resist. With his arms sliding round her, crushing her body tight against his, her defences were non-existent.

Abruptly he put her from him. 'That's better. That was probably good for both of us,' he said coolly. 'It does us all good to indulge ourselves sometimes.'

'Speak for yourself!' Her eyes blazing, Camilla slapped his face. 'That gave *me* more satisfaction.'

Ruefully he rubbed where she had struck, a gleam of devilment lurking in his eyes. 'So now we're quits. Perhaps we can be civil to each other.'

Camilla refused to take the hand he offered. 'Everything has to be on your terms, doesn't it? Nobody else matters.' She grabbed her jacket from the back of the chair and put it on.

'Don't forget your scarf,' he reminded her.

She snatched it up from the table and stuffed it in her bag.

'It's still raining . . . I'll run you home.'

'No you won't. I'd rather drown.'

He laughed softly. 'I'm sure you would, but I shan't let you.' Holding her firmly by the arm, Ross marched her out of the door.

Neither of them said a word as they drove to Islington, but explosive feelings smouldered beneath the surface. On reaching the flat he pushed open the car door for her. 'I'll forgive your display of temper . . . don't lay awake all night worrying about it, will you?' was his parting shot.

She flung him a glacial look, slammed the car door and walked to the house, head high.

Relaxing in her dressing-gown, Marie was watching television. 'Hi! Where've you been?'

'Oh, Ross Noble asked me to call round for my scarf,' Camilla returned offhandedly. 'I had a coffee with him.'

She felt too disturbed to talk about her fight with Ross, even to Marie. And she did lay awake for hours, going over and over it in her mind. The man was absolutely impossible the way he threw his weight about. He was a law unto himself. She didn't know how any woman could put up with him.

His face swam before her. She knew it so well by now. She had watched it often enough with a kind of fascination. There was that habit he had of making direct eye contact when he spoke, the characteristic tightening of his jaw when he was displeased, the tantalising way his lips parted when he smiled. And the memory of those warm, demanding lips on hers had her cheeks burning and her bones melting all over again.

CHAPTER FIVE

WHEN NEXT they met at work, Ross and Camilla were decidedly cool to each other. Accompanying him and Dr Lucy on their ward round, she maintained a strictly professional attitude. She produced case notes when required and drew curtains. She smiled at the patients and at Lucy. But she accorded the registrar only that amount of polite attention which was absolutely necessary.

As always, Mr Bolton was charm itself when they came to see him.

Upon examining his wound, Ross pronounced himself well satisfied. 'Yes, that's nice and healthy. We'll be able to let you go home fairly soon.'

'Splendid.' Mr Bolton took Camilla's hand and squeezed it after she had helped him back into his pyjama jacket. 'You've all been so kind, I can't thank you enough,' he said, including both nurse and doctors in his expression of esteem.

With a half-smile Ross brushed the compliment aside. 'You'll have to take it easy for some time, sir. Give yourself a chance to pick up before you get back into harness,' he warned.

'My wife will see to that, I've no doubt.' Mr Bolton's eyes twinkled. 'The ladies usually get their own way, don't they?'

The registrar gave a wry grin. 'That's debatable . . . there's no harm in letting them think they do. Anyway, I give your wife my support on this occasion.'

Behind his back, Camilla pulled a face at Lucy, who suppressed a smile.

Visiting Fern Debden's room they found her sitting by her bed studying a copy of a play. She looked alluringly feminine in her oyster satin dressing-gown and she threw Ross a coy glance when they entered.

'Will you pop up on the bed for me, Miss Debden?' he asked. 'I'd like to have a look at your tummy.'

'Yes, of course, Doctor.' She fluttered her thick eyelashes at him and arranged herself gracefully on the bed.

Camilla took a loose blanket and draped it over the lower half of the actress's body as she raised her nightie.

Ross inspected the small, healing scar. 'Let me see . . . how long is it now . . . five days?' He picked up the charts from the end of the bed. 'Your stitches can come out in a couple of days. We must complete the course of antibiotics and after that you'll be able to go.'

'I'm booked for a tour of the Midlands in a month.' The actress's eyes were flagrantly seductive as she gazed up in the doctor's face. 'I suppose that will be all right?'

'Yes, it should be fine, provided you're a good

girl and don't overdo things when you leave here,' he said in a strictly parental manner. 'No strenuous exercise for a while.'

Fern's laugh was low and provocative. 'Now what exactly do you mean by that, Doctor?'

He ignored the suggestive inference. 'I leave that to your own good sense.'

Unabashed, she studied the scar on her bikini line. 'It's quite a neat job. But it's as well there are no nude scenes in my next play, isn't it?'

Lucy looked bored and Camilla felt the conversation had gone far enough. She terminated it by pulling down the nightie, saying lightly, 'Well, we'd better leave you to get on with learning your lines.'

'That girl needs her bottom smacked,' Ross drawled when they were out of earshot.

'Is brute force your answer to everything?' asked Camilla smoothly.

'Quite often it's a highly effective measure.'

She gritted her teeth and wished she could have used brute force on him.

They were about to go on to see Miss Whipple when Ross was called to the telephone, after which he and Lucy both left the ward.

Camilla went to tea. On returning she found he was back again on his own, sitting in the office writing up notes.

'Oh, there you are.' He looked up briefly when she came to put her bag in the cupboard. 'I've told Miss Whipple she can go.'

'You're discharging her?' She was surprised. 'Is that wise, considering . . .'

He carried on writing. 'Considering what?'

'Well, everything. I don't know what you've come up with. I only know she's not at all well and that she's got no proper home. There's no one outside to look after her.'

'Your concern is totally misplaced. That woman is a better actress than Fern Debden.'

Camilla frowned. 'What about her pyrexia?'

With a touch of impatience he flung down his pen and darted her a long-suffering glance. 'Really, Nurse, haven't you ever come across temperature faking? Doesn't it strike you as odd that her papers can't be traced when she's had so much surgery?'

'What? Oh!' Camilla caught his drift. 'You mean . . . you think she's a Munchausen?'

'I don't think . . . I know. I was sure I'd seen her before somewhere. I rang the Regional Authority in York, since that's the place she came from. It appears she was in one of their hospitals recently, complaining of a totally different set of symptoms. They rumbled her too. She's already cost the country thousands in unnecessary operations and treatments.'

'Oh dear.' Camilla was momentarily lost for words. 'She had me fooled.'

'Yes, you are inclined to be gullible, aren't you?'

She let that pass. 'I suppose these people are really to be pitied.'

'Save your pity for the patients with genuine

complaints who can't be admitted because the Miss Whipples of this world are occupying the beds,' he retorted.

'You're very unfeeling. She's a pathetic creature . . .'

'I'm so unfeeling that I'm putting her in touch with the social worker and making an appointment for her with a psychiatrist,' he said dryly. 'Which is more than the last place did. They just kicked her out. What do you think I should do? Pat her on the shoulder and say "There! there! never mind"?'

She knew he was right. Camilla sighed. 'I can't help feeling a bit sorry for her.'

His severe expression softened a little. 'You must try to be more realistic. We can't help her, but a psychiatrist may be able to. Get her to call in at the social worker's office for the letter . . . I'll leave it there.'

When Camilla went to deliver the message she found Amy Whipple in a hostile frame of mind, packing her belongings. '*He* says they can't find anything wrong with me . . . well, what does 'e know? 'E ain't got my pain, has he?'

'He's decided you should see another doctor, Miss Whipple. This isn't the right ward for you. If you'll come to the office when you're ready to go I'll get one of the nurses to take you over to the social worker. She's there to help you.'

The buzz had gone round the staff. 'You don't mean to say she was faking, that she actually *enjoys* having operations?' said pupil-nurse Sally, who had never come across such a thing before.

'It's attention-seeking,' Camilla explained. 'It's a way of getting people to notice their existence. They're pitiful cases, but they waste an awful lot of time and money if they're not found out.'

Julian rang her on the ward later that evening. 'I'm free tonight, Ginger, if you are. What about a drink together?'

She hesitated for a moment. Marie had gone home for days off and would not be back till later. She felt like some light relief after dealing with Amy Whipple's problems. Julian was good company. He didn't take himself seriously, or anyone else.

'All right,' she said. 'Where shall I meet you? In A & E?'

'Fine. I'll be in the office.'

Finishing her spell of duty, Camilla changed out of uniform and wandered along in search of him. She found the doctor's office empty and had a word with Ken Drew when he appeared in the corridor. 'I'm looking for Julian . . . do you know where he is?'

'Haven't a clue.' Kenny glanced over her shoulder. 'Oh, here he comes now.'

Camilla turned to see both Ross and Julian approaching, talking together. Julian broke off on seeing her, his preoccupied expression lightening. 'Oh! There you are Ginger. Sorry to keep you. Got

side-tracked. Well, good night you lot.' Wrapping
an arm around her, he headed her in the direction
of the residents' Mess.

Privately Camilla was quite pleased that Ross
had seen her go off with Julian. It proved that she
wasn't to be influenced by his opinions, and a streak
of impishness in her was gratified to notice his jaw
tightening again.

'What were you two talking about?' she said.

'Cricket. What else? We're going down for a
practice in the nets tomorrow evening. Got to get
some in before the big match on Sunday. Will you
be coming to cheer us on?'

'Yes, I suppose so. Not that I'm mad on cricket.'

'Ah, but the honour of St Martin's is at stake. We
need all the support we can get. And there'll be a
disco in the evening.'

The Mess was beginning to fill up with off-duty
staff when Julian and Camilla arrived. She stood
and talked with others while he bought the drinks,
after which they seated themselves at one of the
small tables.

'We should lick the pants off the GCH with Ross
batting for us,' Julian prophesied.

'I shouldn't bank on it. Even the England stars
get out first ball sometimes. Anyway, do we have to
talk about Superman?'

'No, we could talk about us.' He grinned at her
wickedly. 'Do you realise I've been here over four
months and we haven't got it together yet?'

She returned his grin. 'If you mean what I think

you mean, hasn't it dawned on you that I don't go in for one-night stands?'

'It doesn't have to be a one-night stand.'

'Oh, come on, Julian. I can't get romantic over someone who calls me Ginger.'

He pressed a forefinger on her nose. 'Then why did you agree to meet me?'

'Because I was bored and I like your company. Let's settle for being mates.'

He accepted her point of view with good grace and they carried on gossiping in a light-hearted manner.

The mess was getting crowded and presently she noticed Ross come in with Lucy Greene. Camilla found her eyes constantly straying in their direction. With the registrar there it was impossible to keep her mind on Julian.

'It's getting hot in here,' she said. 'Like to come back to my place for a coffee?'

'You mean you actually trust me? I could be a latent werewolf!' Julian snapped his teeth and made a pretend bite towards her neck.

She laughed. 'With any luck Marie will be home. Come on, let's go.'

As they left, she knew that Ross's critical gaze followed them.

Back at the flat Marie arrived home shortly after they did. She produced a cake which her mother had made and they tucked into that, chatting and listening to records before they finally kicked Julian out.

Camilla would really have enjoyed her week in charge of the ward had it not been for her cold war with Ross. The nurses were a good team and got on well together. The registrar was perfectly pleasant with the rest of the staff, she noticed with some resentment. She couldn't understand why he should always single her out for the rough end of his tongue.

With Miss Whipple gone, a patient awaiting surgery was able to be transferred from a medical ward. Mrs Trent was due for removal of a kidney stone but when she was brought over her notes and X-rays were inadvertently left behind.

Coming with Lucy Greene to examine the patient, Ross was put out to find all the details not to hand.

'How am I expected to proceed without them?' he demanded of Camilla.

'I have sent for them,' she returned levelly. 'They shouldn't be long.'

He shot her a dark look from under his frowning brows but turned a winning smile on the patient. 'Well, Mrs Trent, I shall have to come back to see you later,' he said, and strode off.

Lucy grimaced at Camilla before hurrying after her boss, her white coat flapping around her ankles.

Mrs Trent was a timid little woman. 'Is he always that impatient?' she asked.

'No, he's usually very nice. Someone or something must have put him out,' smiled Camilla. That *someone* was most likely to be herself, she thought gloomily.

The registrar returned later, his mood still far from peaceable. 'Where's Mrs Trent's fluid chart?' he wanted to know.

'It's being made up, I expect. She's just used a bedpan,' Camilla said.

'Why is it that nothing's ever in the right place when I want it? I suppose it's too much to ask if you could find me a sphyg?'

'Not at all. I'll get one for you.' She was determined to keep her cool. 'The big white chief wants this,' she said, retrieving the instrument from Sally who was using it. 'I'll let you have it back when he's done with it.'

She took it to him where he was sitting at Mrs Trent's bedside, talking to her quite amiably. 'Here you are. May I wait while you use it?'

Without answering, he wrapped the sleeve around the patient's arm, pumped it up and checked her blood pressure. Then with a brief, 'Thank you,' he handed back the sphygmomanometer without so much as a glance.

'Is there anything else you need?'

'I'll call you if I do.'

Returning the equipment to Sally, she muttered to herself, '*Blow your whistle and we'll all come running.*'

The delivery of controlled drugs had arrived. After signing for them, Camilla was in the process of putting them away when Ross came back to the office. She carried on with her work while he busied himself on the telephone and wrote out some forms.

'Right,' he said, on seeing that she had finished. 'Perhaps you'll give me your attention. Mrs Trent is to have a chest X-ray this afternoon . . . there's the request form. I also want her to have a couple of glycerine suppositories this evening. Push fluids for the rest of the day. We'll be calling for her around one tomorrow so she could have an early morning drink, but no later than six. Is that clear?'

'Perfectly. Are you removing the kidney, or just the stone?'

'It'll be a partial nephrectomy. And *why* are you scowling at me?'

'Me scowling at you? I thought it was the other way around. But I must say that I do take exception to your manner lately.'

'There's nothing wrong with my manner. I'm here to treat patients, not to chat up the staff.'

'Huh! That seems to apply only to me,' she retorted.

'You flatter yourself if you think I give you a second thought, Camilla. And do put on a prettier face. Petulance doesn't become you.'

'I find that rich, coming from you!' She left him quickly as her lips began to tremble. In the kitchen she blew her nose and made an effort to compose herself. What a fool she was to let him provoke her. If only she could be laid back, like Marie, and not take things to heart so much. The trouble was that deep down she knew she wanted Ross to like her. The persistent tension between them troubled her more than she cared to admit.

Stephen phoned her late that night and she was really pleased to hear from him. Still smarting under Ross Noble's animosity, it was a pleasure to talk to someone who wanted to be nice to her.

'I'm coming up to town in the morning,' Stephen said. 'I'd love to see you. What about Saturday afternoon?'

'Oh! I'm working late on Saturday. Sorry, Steve. What a pity.'

'All right. How about tomorrow afternoon then? I'll have a few hours to spare.'

'Well, I am off at four-thirty. We could meet then if you like.'

'Great. Would it be quickest if I were to pick you up at the hospital?'

'Yes, that would be fine. Wait for me by the statue in the square. You can't miss it.'

He was there waiting when she came off duty. 'Hope you don't mind about the dog-collar,' he said, 'but I have to go straight on to a meeting later. I see what you mean about this place,' he went on, 'there is an atmosphere that kind of gets you. I've been watching people coming and going . . . it's a world of its own, isn't it?'

'Would you like a quick tour?' she offered. 'Although I can't take you into the wards . . .'

He said that he would, and she took him around,

pointing out the vast number of departments and the facilities for visitors. Then she showed him the library, the impressive Great Hall lined with portraits of past eminent medical men and lastly the old and beautiful hospital chapel.

He consulted his watch. 'Sadly, I have to be back in Westminster by eight-thirty, much as I'd prefer to spend the rest of the evening with you. Is there somewhere near where we can get a bite to eat, Camilla?'

'Yes, there are places at the Barbican. Come on, we'll go across the walkway and we can have something at the Lakeside Café.'

He tucked an arm through hers and they strolled in the warm evening sunlight towards the Centre. She paused to point out the dome of St Paul's Cathedral in the distance and various other landmarks in the City.

A tall, lithe figure overtook them and turned to look back for a moment. 'Good evening, Camilla,' came Ross Noble's deep voice. He acknowledged her with a brief wave of his hand before striding on.

'Who was that?' Stephen asked.

'Our senior surgical registrar.'

He stroked his beard and smiled wryly. 'I can see I'm outclassed. You'll have no time for rustics with virile specimens like that around.'

'That one's so wrapped up in his work he wouldn't know one end of a girl from the other!' she scoffed.

'No man is that blind. You'd be surprised what goes on in our devious little minds.'

Camilla laughed. 'Maybe I wouldn't.' They had arrived on the lakeside terrace. It had a festive air with its chairs and tables under continental-style sunshades. 'Isn't this nice?' she said. 'We can get something in the restaurant and bring it out here.'

With cool salads, brioche and coffee, they spent a pleasant hour watching the ducks and the lights on the water. By talking generalities, Camilla managed to keep the conversation on an impersonal basis and at length they made their way to the Underground where their ways parted company.

'Well, a pity it's been such a short meeting. I've enjoyed it all the same. Even though I know you've been keeping me at arm's length,' Stephen quipped. He kissed her affectionately. 'Bye, Camilla.'

'Give my love to my folks,' she said.

Most people who were free crowded down to the Sports Ground on Sunday for the cricketing challenge match with the GCH. Marie and Luke had gone down for the day, but Camilla was working until four-thirty. However, Sister Hunter was back on duty at lunch-time and after she had caught up with events on the ward she let Camilla leave earlier.

Going back to the flat she showered, put on a turquoise cotton sundress and set off in her Mini towards the sports ground. Half-way there,

Camilla noticed the red warning light flicking on and off in her instrument panel. Apt to forget things like oil and water, for safety's sake she stopped at the next garage to top up.

Arriving at the ground at six o'clock she found the match nearing its end. She spotted Marie and Luke sitting on the boundary line with a crowd from St Martin's and went over to join them.

'Hi!' Marie greeted her excitedly. 'It's nail-biting time. We need twenty more to win . . . and there's only one more man to go in.'

Camilla flopped on the grass beside her.

'Is that Ross batting?' She knew full well that it was. There was no mistaking that powerful stance and thick tawny hair.

'Yes, he's held the side together,' put in Luke admiringly. 'He's just got his fifty.'

The score went up in singles. The ninth man was caught out and the St Martin's crowd groaned. Last man in was Julian. They needed eight to win. They took two more singles. Then Ross gave the next delivery a mighty whack. It went for six. The home crowd roared with delight as stumps were drawn and the teams made for the clubhouse.

There was a great amount of good-natured ribaldry as the evening festivities got under way, the GCH challenging St Martin's to a return match at their own ground. Most of the team had come by minibus and so they were able to celebrate in due style. Julian was in high spirits, having bowled out a couple of the opposition. Pleased with himself, he grew progressively exuberant. Camilla was rather glad she was not dependent on him for a lift home.

When the disco got underway even Ross joined in, bopping with the best of them. Why can't he always be like that? Camilla thought, hearing his infectious laughter and watching his supple limbs. If he were she might even find herself falling for him.

As the night wore on it grew very warm in the clubhouse, despite open doors and windows. After a strenuous dancing session Camilla wandered out on to the veranda for a breath of air. There was a silver crescent of a moon in the black, star-studded sky, and she stayed to admire it for awhile. The cool air fanned her warm skin and gently ruffled her bright hair.

She was thinking about going in when Ross's powerful figure blocked the doorway. Her pulse began to race and she was caught between the desire to run and the desire to stay. Hesitating, she drew a steadying breath and said, 'Hallo. Lovely out here, isn't it?'

He came and propped his tight buttocks against the balustrade, letting his perceptive blue eyes rove over her bare shoulders. 'You'll get chilled,' he said.

'That's why I came out, to cool off.' She smiled at him. 'I saw your winning six. Well done.'

He dismissed it with a careless shrug. 'Team effort, wasn't it?'

'Yes, I suppose so.'

There was a long silence, during which she didn't quite know where to look, conscious of his steady gaze still weighing her up. She always felt so unsure of herself where he was concerned. She was desperate to have him think well of her and yet, perversely, she wanted to give the impression she didn't care a button what he thought.

'Well,' she said at last, checking her watch, 'it's time I was on my way.'

'Who's taking you home? Julian?'

'No. I came in my own car.'

'Oh!' He paused. 'I noticed you'd extended your favours in another direction. Does the clergy have preference now?'

She remembered he had seen her with Stephen and she bridled at the taunt. 'That was a family friend . . . my father's curate, actually.'

In the subdued light she could not exactly see his expression. 'Ah!' he said.

'Ah, what?'

'I was wondering if you'd had second thoughts with regard to a certain casualty officer.'

'Why don't you mind your own business,' she flashed. 'My private life is no concern of yours.'

'Point taken. Go ahead and make a mess of it.'

'Oh, for goodness' sake! What the hell's the matter with you? Why are you always so rotten to me? Jealous or something?'

His chin jutted in that obstinate way she had come to recognise as dangerous. 'I admit your physical attractions,' he rapped out, 'but I've no intention of letting a woman ruin my life. Have no fears on that score.'

There was a knot in her throat. She swallowed, trying not to let him see her distress. 'You're blinkered,' she said in a choked voice. 'If somebody gave you a bad time I'm sorry. But that's no reason for you to want to spoil it for other people. Leave me out of it!' With her chin in the air, she pushed past him back into the clubhouse.

Most people were now preparing to go home and Julian came towards her, cricket bag in hand. 'I've been looking for you. Want a lift back in the minibus? You can sit on my knee.'

'Thanks, Julian, but I've got my car,' she said.

'Okay, Ginger.' He pushed his face forward for a kiss. 'Mind how you go.'

Five minutes later she left with Marie and Luke who set out in their own car just ahead of her.

Once on her own behind the wheel, Camilla battled with a whole gamut of emotions as she thought about her latest encounter with Ross. Anger, frustration and self-pity were mixed up with a kind of wonderment at his admission.

Did he really say he found her physically attractive? Well, the same thing applied equally in reverse, heaven help her, except that it wasn't only his physique which appealed to her. When he was not behaving like a tetchy tiger she caught fascinating glimpses of the man who, more and more, threatened her peace of mind. For no justifiable reason he was constantly invading her thoughts. It was something she would have to conquer since they seemed destined to do nothing but fight.

There was not a great deal of passing traffic as she bowled along the country road heading for London. She had completely lost sight of Marie and Luke. She had barely gone five miles when her red warning light came on again and kept flashing. About the same time she also began to notice a smell of burning rubber. *Oh help!* she thought, *I must be overheating.*

Pulling to a stop on the hard shoulder, she opened up the bonnet and shone her torch inside. Not that she knew much about the inner workings of engines, but the heat that shot out at her would have told any novice that something was wrong.

This on top of everything else! She could have howled. Leaving the bonnet open to cool, she collected her shoulder-bag from the car and set off to hike back to the telephone point she had passed about a mile back.

The white Jaguar caught up with her as she was half-way. Ross wound down the window. 'Hallo. What's the trouble?'

Anyone was welcome at that moment, mortified though she was that it should be him. 'My engine seems to be packing up. I'm on my way to the phone.'

'Hop in,' he invited. 'I'll have a look at it. Might be something simple.'

Within a few minutes he had pulled up behind

her Mini. She held the torch for him while he inspected the works. It took him no time at all to discover the problem. 'You've got a broken fan belt. Have you a spare?'

'Oh, no . . . I haven't.'

'Typical. Well, mine won't fit. And you won't find a spares garage open at this time of night.'

'Then I'd better phone the AA hadn't I?'

He considered. 'Hmmm . . . you could be waiting hours. I've got a tow-rope. Be best if I give you a tow.'

From the boot of his car he produced a nylon cable and linked their vehicles together.

'We ought to have a notice on the back. Have you got a lipstick?' She searched in her bag and found one for him. He scrawled ON TOW in large letters on a folder from among his papers and fastened it to the rear of the Mini.

'I'm terribly sorry to give you so much trouble.'

He looked at her from under his level brows. 'I enjoy heaping coals of fire.'

She gave a sheepish grin. 'I bet you do.'

'Right. Let's get going or we shan't be home before the milk.'

He drove very steadily. It was an odd feeling being pulled along with no power of her own. At traffic lights he glanced back to make sure all was well. Camilla watched the back of his head and wondered why even the set of his shoulders could cause a rumpus inside her. She thought about his complex personality; tough yet considerate, abrasive yet beguiling. I'd rather have you for a friend than an enemy, she decided.

It was nearly two by the time they pulled up outside the Islington flat. Luke's car was there.

'Thank you once again,' Camilla said when Ross untied the tow-rope and put it away. She flashed him a smile of relief mixed with impudence. 'If I asked you in for a drink would you think I'd got designs on you?'

He raised a self-mocking eyebrow. 'I think you've made the opposite plain enough.'

'Would you like a coffee then?'

'Aren't you afraid my animal instincts will get the better of me?'

'Oh, I'd be quite safe,' she returned pertly, 'Marie and Luke are back.'

'Otherwise you wouldn't have offered! Thanks for the compliment.' Getting into his own car, he slammed the door and drove off.

Camilla sighed. I've done it again! she thought. Letting herself into the house, disconsolately she went upstairs. The other couple were sitting on the sofa in the living-room, looking at literature from house agents.

'You've been a long time. We were beginning to get worried about you,' Marie said.

She explained what had happened. 'I'd probably be stuck on the road even now if Ross hadn't come along.' Cross with herself at having annoyed him again, she had to do something before she burst into tears. 'I'll make coffee. Want another one?'

Marie followed her out into the kitchen. 'That was decent of him, wasn't it? Why didn't you ask him in?'

Camilla let out a long exasperated breath. 'I did!' she said through clenched teeth. 'But we're agreed on mutual antipathy. That man! He makes me sick, he's so damned difficult.'

'Don't get so steamed up about things,' said Marie with a light laugh.

'Well, I can't help it. That's me.'

'Perhaps he was just feeling tired. After all, it has been a hectic day.'

'Oh, stop making excuses for him. I refuse to bow to his inflated ego.'

When the coffee was made she said good night to the others and carried hers through to her room, where at last she could indulge in the luxury of tears. It was hateful, being obligated to him. But in spite of their differences, Camilla realised only too well that Ross could have her in the palm of his hand if he chose. Sadly he showed no signs of even liking her, let alone loving her. And she would die rather than let him know how she felt.

CHAPTER SIX

MR BOLTON said his goodbyes to the staff of Simpson Ward. Aided by crutches he had learned to walk quite well with the heel on his plastered foot, and his nephrectomy wound had healed satisfactorily.

Thanking them all for their care and attention, he added, 'I won't forget about the barbecue. I'll be in touch as soon as we fix something up.'

His son, who had come to collect him, handed Jean Hunter two bottles of sherry. 'Meantime,' he said, 'we thought you'd like to celebrate his departure.' Looking very elegant in black leather trousers and a cream sweater, Dominic had a special smile for Camilla as he shook hands with her before leaving. 'I hope we shall meet again,' he said.

A little earlier Fern Debden had also left on the arm of one of her admirers, and the ward blossomed with the flowers she had left behind. Despite her affectations she had been an interesting patient and had brought a touch of glamour to the ward.

'She really fancied herself, but I couldn't help liking her,' Camilla said.

Jean agreed. 'I wouldn't care for her life-style

though. It must be tough having to show a charming face to the world all the time, especially when you're feeling anything but. I'll settle for being ordinary.'

She had returned from her holiday in a contented frame of mind. 'Duncan has got his shore job at Head Office all lined up,' she confided to Camilla. 'We'll be getting married after his next trip.'

'Oh, that's great! Have you decided where you'll live?'

'In my flat to begin with. It'll be convenient for him and I don't plan to leave here yet awhile.' About to go off duty, Jean rolled down her sleeves, buttoned her cuffs and took her handbag from the cupboard. 'We're going to have the service in the chapel here and the reception in the Great Hall if it can be arranged. I've got a date with the chaplain now.'

'It must be the mating season,' Camilla said smiling. 'There's my flatmate Marie hoarding like a demented squirrel. Whenever she goes shopping she comes home with some new kitchen gadget. It'll be baby clothes next, I shouldn't wonder.'

Jean laughed. 'We may have left it a bit late for that, but you never know.'

Teas had been served to the patients and, while waiting for the end of visiting, Camilla had been teaching Sally how to lay up a dressings trolley. Anaesthetist Larry Woodford arrived and looked in on them.

'Hallo,' he said, his manner shy and friendly as always. 'May I see your two patients for tomorrow's list?'

Camilla liked Larry. He was a quiet, unassuming man in his mid-thirties.

'Yes. There's Mr Williams, varicose veins, and Mr Meredith, double inguinal hernia. Like a cup of tea first? Visitors will be leaving in a few minutes.'

'Thanks.' He followed her into the kitchen and watched while she boiled the kettle and made the tea. 'Expect you know I'm leaving at the end of the week.'

She nodded. 'Marie told me. I'm really sorry. We shall miss you.'

'I bet you say that to everyone,' he returned with a modest smile.

'Oh, no I don't. Where are you going?'

'To Bangladesh. Doing my bit for the third world. I'm having farewell drinks in my flat on Friday, if you'd like to come.'

'Love to.' She poured the tea and they carried it through to the office. 'Had you said Saturday I couldn't have made it. I'm starting nights.'

'Does that mean you'll miss the great return cricket spectacular?'

'Probably. I kind of hibernate on night duty.' She glanced at her watch and rang the bell to clear the ward.

Larry finished his drink and got up to see his patients.

'George Meredith is asthmatic,' Camilla reminded him, showing him to the bay which housed the two new patients, 'but he's had no trouble since he's been in here.'

Leaving him to his work, Camilla wished her relationship with Ross were as easy. There had been only fleeting contact between them so far that week. Ward rounds had been accompanied by either Jean Hunter or one of the other staff nurses. He had made a point once of enquiring whether she'd managed to get her car fixed and she had told him that so far she hadn't.

His manner had been civil enough then, but whenever she saw him it unsettled her. Peculiar sensations ran down her spine. She felt tense and apprehensive. Much the same kind of fluttery feeling that gripped her before any important event in her life. Silly really, because he was never going to matter to her, or she to him, even though he had said she attracted him physically. She wondered what actually went through his mind when he looked at her in that inscrutable manner.

On Friday evening she arrived at Larry's party a little after nine. People were dropping in and out as their duties allowed. Ken Drew was there and taking quite a lively interest in Lucy who, for all her lack of size, was good company. Julian, too, was in ebullient mood as usual and waxing lyrical about the forthcoming return cricket contest.

'How can you get so excited about hitting a ball with a lump of wood?' Camilla teased him.

'Woman, that's heresy!' he declared. 'Sex apart, there's no other decent topic of conversation.'

'That's my father's pet subject too,' Lucy put in. 'I hoped I'd heard the last of silly-mid-offs when I left home.'

'Cross my heart and hope to die, I shall never bore you with the subject, Lucy,' smiled Ken.

Camilla wondered if that might be the next romance at St Martin's. She saw Ross arrive in the company of a stranger. He was apparently in a good humour and after talking to Larry for some time, he brought the newcomer over to meet them.

'Do you know Bob Bannister? He's taking Larry's place,' Ross said.

The new anaesthetist, a brown-haired man with owlish glasses and an earnest manner, shook hands solemnly with them all. When introduced, he repeated their names as though intent on committing them to memory. Camilla found herself thinking that anaesthetists seemed to be a distinctive breed. Perhaps putting people to sleep was a chastening occupation which discouraged frivolity.

Ross was again unusually polite to her. Since their last blow up a kind of truce appeared to be operating. But she was surprised when, later on, out of the blue he said: 'I picked up a new fan belt for you. Would you like me to come over and fit it on?'

It caught her off-guard. She smiled at him. 'That's very sweet of you.'

'I've been called a few things in my time, but

never sweet before,' he returned wryly.

'Maybe I'm beginning to see the better side of your nature.'

'You think I might have one?'

'Life's full of surprises. When could you . . . I mean, when would you like to do it?'

'No time like the present. I've got the car outside. Shall we go now?'

'Oh. All right. I'd better say goodbye to Larry first.'

She also stopped to tell Julian she was leaving. 'And don't think I'm boycotting your cricket match. I'm going on to nights so I won't be around for awhile.'

He ran a finger down her spine. 'Okay, Ginger. I'll forgive you. If you like to hang on for ten minutes I'll take you home.'

'That's all right. Ross is driving me.'

'Oh. Deserting me for him, are you?'

'No. My fan belt busted last weekend. He's offered to fit me a new one.'

Julian threw back his head and laughed. 'That's a novel approach. Perhaps I should fix your chastity belt first.'

'You', she said with a grin, 'are incorrigible. I'm in no danger from him. We're agreed on being friendly enemies.'

She stopped to say good night to a few more folk before rejoining Ross, who waited with ill-concealed impatience. 'I thought you were never coming,' he growled.

So the lull in hostilities hadn't lasted long. 'Sorry, but I had to say goodbye to people. If it's inconvenient, don't bother. I can go home by train.'

His shrewd blue eyes bored into hers. 'The last train's probably gone by now, so stop airing your independence and come along.'

He could well be right about the trains, she decided. She didn't want to go back to Julian. She might have got a taxi, or kipped down on someone's floor, but that seemed a bit petty after his offer. Swallowing her pride she went along with him.

They drove in silence for a few minutes. When she could stand it no longer, she said, 'Why do you bother with me if you find me such a pain?'

His lips twitched. 'Ask me another. Freud might know the answer to that, but not a simple man like me.'

'Simple? You are the most complicated man I have ever met.'

'Indeed? Well, that makes two of us. So shall we call it a draw?'

Camilla sighed. 'I'm not out to score points. All I want is a quiet life, which seems to be asking the impossible.' She changed the subject. 'Do you know a lot about cars?'

'Fan belts aren't too difficult, provided you've got the right tools.'

'I'd have had to get a garage to come out and do it.'

'So I'll save you a few pennies, won't I?' He

pulled up behind her Mini, which was still parked outside the flat, where he had left it after towing her. 'If you'll release your bonnet catch it shouldn't take me long.'

She unlocked the car and did as he asked. Then she watched while he worked, admiring his bent head and wanting to run her fingers through his thick fair hair. He fiddled capably with spanners and nuts. 'I wonder why men are more mechanically-minded than women?' she said.

'There are some things women are better at than men. They should stick to their proper role.'

'That's a sexist thing to say. I suppose you think they should stay home and look after the kids.'

'Don't put words in my mouth. Some jobs demand brawn as well as brain. Pass me the new fan belt.'

She handed it over. Tightening a nut, he knocked a finger, cursed mildly under his breath and sucked it for a moment.

'Should you really be doing this?' she ventured.

'Why ever not?'

'Well, I mean, I wouldn't like you to ruin your hands on my account.'

'One can't go through life avoiding getting hurt.'

'Oh,' she said, innocently, 'I thought that was what you were trying to do?'

He lifted his head long enough to give her a straight look, then carried on working. Having finished at last, he wiped his hands on a rag. 'There you are. You'll need to get it tightened once it's run in.'

'Thanks. Thanks very much.' She caught the faint bleep-bleep-bleep of his intercom coming from the Jaguar, and nodded her head in that direction. 'It sounds as if you're wanted.'

He let out a weary sigh. 'Mind if I use your phone?'

'No, of course not.' Opening the front door, she ran upstairs ahead of him. There was no one else at home. She pointed Ross in the direction of the telephone and he dialled the hospital number.

'That was the houseman in Casualty; there's a query perforated duodenal ulcer,' he told her after a brief conversation. 'Oh dear!' He inspected his grubby hands and the oily marks on the white handpiece he had just put down. 'Sorry, I seem to have made this dirty.'

'That's okay. Would you like to wash?'

She showed him where the bathroom was. Presently he had gone, leaving her with an absurd feeling of anticlimax. How might the evening have ended, she wondered, if he had not been called back to the hospital? She had been thinking of asking him in for a drink, but even if he'd accepted, they might have finished up arguing over some trifling thing again. At least this time they had parted without rancour. She hoped it might be the beginning of better relations between them.

Camilla's thoughts followed him to the hospital. She saw him putting on his surgeon's face, weighing up facts and making clinical judgments with that clearness of vision which inspired confidence in patients and staff alike. It couldn't be easy having to switch from private to professional matters at the drop of a hat. It could well create havoc with personal relationships. And judging by things he had let drop, that was possibly the cause of his failed love affair.

Meantime, she herself had two whole days off to look forward to, with no fear of interruption, before starting nights. For a whole month she would very likely not even set eyes on him. The notion left a hollow feeling inside her. It was as if a vital force had suddenly switched off, leaving her in limbo, without motivation. She had not realised how much he had come to occupy her thoughts of late. And that was lunatic, considering he had said he didn't intend any woman to figure largely in his life again. But he might at least get to like her a little bit, mightn't he? she mused wistfully.

Annoyed with herself for caring whether he did or not, she endeavoured to put him out of mind. Even so, he continued to haunt her far into the night.

Marie was also off for the weekend. With Luke away on a management course, the following day the two girls had an enjoyable shopping spree in the West End. Inevitably Marie was drawn to the bridal departments in the big stores, and they both drooled over dreamy creations in gorgeous fabrics.

'The price of them!' Marie exclaimed, admiring

an ethereal gown with a fine lace trimming. 'Good job my dad is going to pay.'

'But you won't buy it yet, will you?' Camilla said.

'No. I want to try and lose a bit of weight first.'

'You could take up jogging. Or better still, why don't we join an aerobics class? June Finch goes to one. She says it's great.'

In anticipation, they both bought leotards and leg warmers, planning to ask June about the class. They finished up having a pizza in an Italian café before going on to see a film.

'You are lucky, having a nice guy like Luke,' Camilla said with a touch of envy.

'I know I am.' Marie sighed blissfully. 'I really don't know what he sees in me. I mean, no matter how much I diet I'll never be a Twiggy, will I? I'm an endomorph.'

Camilla laughed. 'It takes all sorts . . . some men prefer the cuddly kind. Funny, isn't it, what makes two people click. The eternal enigma.'

The romantic film they saw proved her point. The heroine and hero were locked in conflict for most of the time, although love triumphed in the end. All very well on the silver screen, she thought sadly, but in real life it was sheer hell to be constantly at odds with someone who had only to look at you to make your heart leap.

Changing over from days to nights, which happened every four months, always presented something of a problem for Camilla. She usually opted for staying up late the night before so that she would be tired enough to want a few hours rest the following afternoon. But it always took time to adjust her sleep pattern.

At eight-thirty on Monday evening she received the report from Matty Newbury, who was now on days.

'There's Miss Garland, sixty, in High Dependency. She came in on Friday night straight from theatre . . . perforated duodenal ulcer. Nothing by mouth yet. She's on four-hourly naso-gastric feeds and hourly gastric aspirations. She's still quite poorly.'

Camilla's mind registered that this must have been Ross's emergency of the other night.

Going through the rest of the patients, Matty went on, 'George Meredith had a bout of asthma after his visitors had left. We gave him Ventolin in the nebuliser, which seems to have worked. He's had his Intal tonight, but I'd keep an eye on him.'

The day staff left and the night staff began their busy evening round. On duty with Camilla were SRN Pamela, a quiet married part-timer, and third-year student Joyce, a happy-go-lucky twenty-one-year old.

Joyce collected the late-night drink beakers, sped round with bottles and bedpans and did the observations. Camilla and Pam did the drug round and made ill patients comfortable.

Dealing with Miss Garland first, they found a painfully thin lady who did indeed look poorly.

There was a flush on her high cheek-bones and her appearance was not enhanced by the naso-gastric tube taped in position.

'Hallo, Miss Garland,' Camilla said in a soft voice. 'How are you feeling tonight?'

'Not too bad, dear. Better than I did. I'll be glad when I can have a drink though.'

'You will tomorrow, probably. There's not much coming from your naso-gastric tube now, so you'll be getting rid of that soon. Now, put your hands on your tummy and roll over to me while Pam does your back.'

When they had finished treating her pressure areas and smoothing the draw sheet, Camilla said, 'We'll give you a mouth wash . . . that'll freshen you up.'

'Oh, that would be nice, dear,' said Miss Garland gratefully. 'You're good girls.'

It was after eleven before the last sedative had been given and the last patient settled for the night. Pam and Joyce retired to sluice and kitchen to tidy up, complete fluid charts and label specimens. Camilla turned down the lights except for those shaded over the beds of the more ill patients, and lowered the lamp over the nurses' station.

Night Sister arrived to do her first round. 'No problems, Nurse Clifton?' She was a well-upholstered, fussy woman in her fifties, a product of the old school who liked all bed castors facing inwards, locker tops kept tidy, and pillow ends facing one way.

'Everything's fine so far, Sister,' Camilla said. On soft-soled shoes she walked quietly round the darkened ward with her senior, who personally checked that drips were running as they should be.

The sister stopped to scold a patient who was indulging in a sly smoke. She helped to prop up George Meredith who had slipped down the bed and was beginning to wheeze again. 'Try to keep up, Mr Meredith,' she said briskly. 'You'll feel better if you do.' Everything to her satisfaction, she went on to her next ward.

'I've made coffee,' said Joyce, and the three nurses sat down around the desk for the first respite of the evening.

A patient quietly padded off towards the toilet and Camilla jumped up to go after her. 'Mrs Trent . . . use a bedpan and leave it there, will you? We have to measure it.'

'Yes, dear,' Mrs Trent said in a stage whisper, 'I hadn't forgotten.'

Somewhere in the corridors a lift-gate clanged. In the distance an ambulance siren wailed. Other than that only a few odd grunts and snores broke the silence.

With daytime activities at a standstill and no traffic of medics and technicians, a different atmosphere prevailed in the quiet wards. Very sick patients developed special attachments for the nurses who ministered to them in the small hours, while among the staff there grew a special kind of relationship with confidences exchanged and jokes shared in hushed voices.

At one a.m. Pam went off for her meal break, leaving Camilla with the student. Sitting in the pool of light at the desk, Camilla made a few preliminary notes for her handover report in the morning.

Joyce, glancing through a nursing magazine in a tired fashion, yawned. 'I didn't sleep too well yesterday. They're digging up the road outside my flat. I can usually sleep through anything, but it was so warm, wasn't it?'

'Yes, no air about. I shan't be sorry when my first night's over, either.' Camilla glanced up with a frown as a sound of coughing reached her ears. 'Think that's Mr Meredith.' She went to check that he was all right. After giving him a drink of water she turned his pillow and he seemed to settle. But the coughing had awakened other patients and there was a spate of requests for bedpans.

Things quietened down once more. Joyce started on the two a.m. observations while Camilla aspirated Miss Garland's naso-gastric tube. Then Mr Meredith's cough started up again in real earnest. He started to retch with the effort.

Quickly Camilla finished what she was doing and hurried to his bedside. He lay back against his pillow exhausted and anxious. She wiped his sweaty face and reached for the oxygen mask. 'Try not to panic, George. This will help while I get you your inhaler.'

Leaving the face mask in place, she went off to fetch him the inhaler, but by the time she returned he had torn off the mask and was making stertorous noises as he fought for breath.

Promptly Camilla replaced the mask and pressed his call button which brought Joyce to her aid. 'Bleep the houseman,' she murmured urgently. 'He's going to need some i.v. drugs. Then bring a tray with two-fifty mgs aminophylline and two hundred mgs hydrocortisone. Take the keys from my pocket.' She continued to hold the mask over the patient's mouth while Joyce sped off to do the necessary. 'Just try to breathe steadily, George, you're going to be all right,' Camilla reassured him.

It took Lucy about five minutes to arrive. With old slacks and a sweater hastily put on beneath her long white coat, she scurried towards the screened bed. 'Have you some aminophylline there?' she asked.

'Yes, everything's here.' Camilla had the syringe and drug ready and the doctor administered the slow, intravenous injection. She then set up an intravenous drip of hydrocortisone.

Mr Meredith stopped gasping and began to breath more easily. 'That's better,' said Lucy, smiling with relief.

'Thank you,' wheezed George.

She checked that his blood pressure and pulse rate had become more normal. 'We'll let you get some rest now.'

He put out a grateful hand and touched her coat sleeve. 'Thanks again,' he said.

'Would you like a drink, Lucy?' Camilla asked

when they had settled the patient and were going back to the office.

'Yes, please. Not coffee though, or I'll never get off to sleep again. Have you got some cocoa?'

'Cocoa it is.' Camilla made the drink. 'Sorry to drag you out.'

Lucy glanced at the ward clock. It was three a.m. 'Oh well, I'll get another four hours in if I'm lucky.'

Camilla smiled in sympathy. At least nurses did not get called from their beds unless there should happen to be a major disaster.

Pam had by now returned, and with the ward peaceful once more, Camilla and Joyce went off for their own belated meal-break. The rest of the night passed without incident. Soon it was time to wake patients up with early morning tea and start the ritual of washings, medicines and bed-making.

Camilla fell into bed at nine-thirty that morning and slept soundly until five, when Marie came in and regaled her with the latest happenings in theatre that day. 'Ross and Prof Purbright removed a cervical rib. It was pressing on the brachial artery and caused this woman's arm to go numb. They think they've managed to restore circulation. It was really interesting. Ross asked where you were, by the way. I told him you were on nights.'

'Surprised he even noticed my absence,' said Camilla. But she felt a glow of pleasure to know that he had mentioned her. Although she had tried hard to forget about him there was always something to bring him to mind; the casual mention of his name by someone, the sight of his handwriting on case notes. Longing for just a glimpse of him, she found herself even hoping some late-night emergency might bring him to the ward.

It was something of a surprise, however, when the following Sunday night Ross did turn up. It was shortly after ten o'clock. There was nothing amiss on the ward and they had not been advised to expect a new patient.

'Hallo! What brings you here?' she said, her pulse quickening at the sight of him.

He stood waiting while she locked the drugs trolley away. 'I wondered if you'd heard the news?' he said.

She smiled, wondering at a certain solemnity in his voice. 'About the result of the cricket match you mean? No . . . didn't you win?'

Ross shook his head. 'I meant, about Julian Gilmore.'

She sensed that something was wrong. 'Why? What's happened?'

'He was hit on the head with a cricket ball this afternoon. He was fielding close to the wicket and took the full force of it.'

Camilla caught her breath. 'Oh dear!' She could tell by his manner that the injury was serious. 'H-how bad is it?'

'Skull fracture and a major haemorrhage. They took him to Theatre and tried to evacuate the clot. He's on ITU now . . .'

'Oh my God! How awful.' Tears sprang to her

eyes and she bit her lips to stop them quivering.

Ross laid a tentative hand on her shoulder. 'He didn't know much about it, Camilla. He went out like a light.'

She had a mental image of the fun-loving Julian, now lying helpless with tubes and leads attached to his inert body. 'Wh-what's the outlook?' she asked, controlling her voice with difficulty.

'Not good. The brain scan shows irreparable damage.' He paused. 'I'm so sorry. I know how fond you are of him.'

The tragedy of it all made her angry. 'Of course I'm fond of him,' she flared. 'Most people are. He's a lovable bloke.'

'Yes. A great guy. Well . . . I thought you'd want to know.' He seemed reluctant to leave. 'Are you going to be all right? Nothing I can do?'

At the back of her mind it dawned on her that he took her to be personally involved, but it wasn't the moment to put him straight. 'No . . . no, nothing, thanks.'

'Okay. I'm sorry, Camilla. Very sorry. Good night.' He walked slowly away.

Camilla's tears overflowed. She went to the office, blew her nose and tried to compose herself. Pam, noticing her distress, came to ask what was the matter.

'Oh, how ghastly,' she said when Camilla found the words to explain. 'Is he . . . special to you?'

'Not in that way. But he's a lovely guy. We are very good friends.'

'Well, sometimes people do get over these things and confound the experts. Maybe it's not so bad as it sounds,' Pam said encouragingly.

The time dragged on until Night Sister put in an appearance and they could enquire how he was. She spread her hands non-committally. 'Still unconscious, I'm afraid. No change.'

During her meal-break Camilla hurried along to ITU to see for herself and talk with the staff nurse in charge.

'His parents have been sitting with him,' the girl said, 'but I've just persuaded them to go to the relatives' room to try and get some sleep. I mean,' she shrugged, 'there is nothing much anyone can do . . . Come and see.'

Julian lay motionless with his head swathed in bandages. Camilla could hear the soft shunt of the bellows as the life-support machine to which he was attached forced air into his lungs. She watched the monitor recording his heart beats. And her throat ached for him. Oh! It was so unfair that something like this should have happened to a man whose vocation was to save life. A promising career cut short.

In the morning when she went off duty, tired as she was, Camilla felt that she had to go along again to ITU to see whether, by some miraculous chance, there had been any improvement.

Outside Julian's room she met up with June Finch, who shook her head. 'He's not going to make it, Cam,' she sighed. 'His parents are in there with him now. He's their only son.'

'I know,' said Camilla. 'It must be dreadful for them.' The two girls exchanged despairing glances.

'We're just going to turn him,' June said, 'so I'll get them to come out. Perhaps you'd like to talk to them?'

Camilla gulped. 'What will I say?'

'I don't know . . . you'll think of something.' June brought the parents out and introduced them.

'We're all so terribly sorry,' Camilla said in a broken voice. 'Everyone likes Julian.'

The father's eyes were deep pools of anguish.

The mother looked dazed and sank wearily on to a chair. 'We had dinner with him on Saturday evening. I—it doesn't seem possible . . .'

Camilla sat down beside her and held her hand. 'You can be sure that everything possible is being done for him, Mrs Gilmore.' Her words sounded so inadequate, so banal, when their son was lying at death's door. Oh, it was so ironic. Here he was with every facility medical science could offer, in one of the best hospitals in London, and they could do nothing to save him.

It was useless to say things like 'try not to worry' when she knew the situation was hopeless. All she could do was to try and give practical help. She took a firm grip on her own emotions. 'Have you had breakfast yet?'

They shook their heads. 'I couldn't eat a thing,' his mother said.

'You ought to try. Look, come down to the staff

dining-room with me and I'll organise you something. I'm sure you'd feel better for it.'

She managed to persuade them and over toast and coffee they talked about Julian and his work and the high hopes they had had for him.

'Where do you work, dear?' his mother asked.

'I'm on nights on a surgical ward.'

'You've been up all night? Oh, my goodness, you must be tired. You all work so hard. And we're keeping you from your bed.'

'That's all right,' Camilla said. 'I just wish there was something I could do.'

With Julian on her mind, she slept fitfully that day, and when she returned to work in the evening she learned that his condition had worsened.

It was around midnight when Night Sister brought the news that Julian's life had finally flickered out. 'He carried a donor's card, you know. Ross Noble asked his parents' permission all the same.' She gave a heavy sigh. 'It's very difficult, isn't it? Later on I suppose it will help, knowing that someone else lives because of their son, but it is harrowing at the time.'

All who knew the formerly lively young doctor were sick at heart. Camilla had often been called upon to try and bring comfort to bereaved relatives, but she had never before had to come to grips with the death of a personal friend. It was a distressing experience which left a real physical ache inside her. It was some time before she could even think of Julian without weeping.

CHAPTER SEVEN

A MONTH had passed since Julian's fatal accident. The remainder of Camilla's spell of night duty had been like a period of mourning, tinged with deep sadness. Now she gave her last handover report and left the ward, thankful to be returning to normality.

Having worked the last seven days without a break, she had five days off to look forward to and could take full advantage of the continuing fine weather. She celebrated by going across to The Jolly Friars where one could get a sumptuous breakfast of egg, bacon and tomato for a modest sum. It was a haunt of newspaper men as well as the hospital staff, and the place had a welcoming air of relaxation with colleagues gathering together to exchange news and views.

Spotting Ken Drew and Yvonne, one of the theatre nurses, Camilla went to join them after ordering her meal. 'Hi, you two. What's been going on in the real world?'

'Not a lot,' Ken grinned. 'A & E has had its usual quota of drunks, junkies and drop-outs. Actually we were just talking about your Mr Bolton. Sounds a super day he's putting on, doesn't it?'

'Oh, when's that? I haven't heard anything.'

'Marie hasn't told you?' queried Yvonne.

Camilla seasoned her breakfast and broke into her crusty roll. 'No, she wasn't home before I went to work last night.'

'He's putting on a barbecue at his riverside place next Sunday. The invites came yesterday. I should have thought Sister Hunter would have said.'

'Well, she wasn't on last night,' said Camilla, 'and she probably didn't think about it this morning.'

The others told her what they knew of the details. Besides the barbecue there was to be swimming and later, dancing on the lawn or inside if the weather should prove unkind.

'Sounds as if he's going to a lot of trouble,' said Camilla. 'Glad I'll be off duty and able to go.'

'It's a fair distance,' put in Ken, 'but most people have got cars. I'll have a couple of spare seats if you know anyone who needs a lift.'

After finishing her meal, Camilla went home to bed cheered at the prospect of what promised to be an enjoyable day out. When she awoke that evening Marie was home and rather disconsolate that she would have to miss out on the fun. 'I'm on a flipping late,' she said in disgust.

'Oh, what a shame. You can't swop with anyone?'

'I couldn't very well ask. They all want to go, don't they? And someone's got to staff the department. Oh well,' she went on with her usual affability, 'it's only for hospital staff. I'd rather spend the day with Luke if I had it off anyway.'

Jean Hunter rang Camilla later that evening to pass on the news. 'It slipped my mind this morning. You're off, aren't you? Will you be coming?'

'Rather. Sounds fantastic, especially if this weather holds.'

'Well, it seems pointless to take two cars,' Jean said. 'We'll use mine, shall we? I'll pick you up around eleven-thirty.'

London sweltered in the promised warm spell. Heat beat back from pavements and buildings. Shirt sleeves were the order of the day for the City's policemen and the parks abounded with Londoners making the most of the weather during their lunch-break.

Camilla's time off passed quickly. She got together with old friends who had since moved on from St Martin's, and they had a day at the Oasis Pool in Holborn. She went with Marie and June to the aerobics class, finishing up with some of the crowd for drinks at a Covent Garden wine bar.

Towards the end of the week Marie was also free. They took a picnic to Wimbledon and watched the tennis championships, coming home at the end of the day with the beginnings of a tan and sated with sunshine.

Camilla was looking forward tremendously to Sunday and the trip to Maidenhead. She wondered whether Ross would be there. It seemed ages since she had seen him. In fact the last time was that tragic night when he had come to tell her about

Julian. But out of sight had been in no way out of mind. She realised he had come to her out of kindness, obviously believing her to be in love with Julian. She remembered how she had snapped at him because she had been so shocked and sad and how, for the first time in their dealings, he had soft-pedalled with her. It was almost as though he had wanted to stay and comfort her but was at a loss to know how. Maybe he felt a kind of empathy having loved and lost himself. She sighed and wished yet again that she was not so quick to retaliate.

On Sunday morning Camilla showered, shampooed her hair and painted her nails. Her skin glowed from her outdoor activities and the sun had brought out the freckles across her nose and shoulders. She had bought a new summery skirt and a primrose cotton-knit sun-top. Her jewellery was a pair of gold hoop earrings and a thin gold chain to go round her neck. With white strappy sandals on her bare feet, she was ready and waiting for Jean when the front doorbell rang.

Propping a pair of sunglasses across the top of her shiny hair, Camilla picked up her leisure bag packed with swimsuit and towel and ran lightly downstairs.

On the doorstep Jean Hunter waited, looking cool and elegant in a pink linen sleeveless dress, a folded chiffon scarf tying back her long dark hair. But it was not Jean's car which stood in the road. It was the white Jaguar with its sunshine roof open. Ross sat drumming his fingers on the wheel, looking ruggedly attractive in a deep blue open-necked sports shirt with his golden hair fanned by the breeze.

'I thought we were taking your car,' Camilla said to Jean, her breath coming quickly.

'Well, Ross had empty seats, and he knows the way, whereas I don't.'

Camilla's stomach had started to churn. She felt ridiculously uptight as she went with Jean towards the car.

'Hallo,' Ross said, pleasantly enough, pushing open both back and front passenger doors.

'I'll go in the back,' offered Jean. She did so before Camilla could demur.

Ross started up the car, giving Camilla a sideways glance as they set off. 'You look as if you've been soaking up the sun.'

'Yes, I've made the most of it.' How adolescent to be in such a state just because she was sitting next to him. But the close proximity of his strong body had that effect upon her. It was like a magnetic forcefield which trapped her and from which there was no escape. Smoothing damp palms surreptitiously on her skirt, she dragged her eyes away from his fascinating profile and concentrated on the road ahead. 'How long does it take to get there?'

'About an hour, traffic permitting.' He slipped a cassette into the player and gaps in conversation were filled with agreeable background music. Not that Jean was at a loss for words. She chatted easily about a number of things, including the exciting arrangements for her wedding at the end of July.

'We'll have to work the off-duty so that you can come,' she said.

Ross wove his way skilfully through the London traffic, across the Hammersmith flyover to join the motorway, contributing the odd remark when he was not too occupied.

Soon they were out into the softly rolling landscape of Berkshire. From time to time there were glimpses of the Thames. It flowed past picturesque islands, weirs and locks, while launches, skiffs and canoes were busy on its calm waters. Mansions with trim lawns sloped down to the banks and restaurant gardens were gay with umbrellas. Ross pointed out Boulter's Lock where a variety of pleasure craft waited to pass through.

'Oh yes, that's *Three Men in a Boat* country, isn't it?' Camilla said, recalling one of the books set for her 'A' level English during schooldays.

They reached a tree-shaded drive with *Mulberry Court* on a rustic sign at the entrance, where Ross turned in.

'I've passed this place a number of times but never thought I should be coming here.'

It was a long drive, opening out eventually to landscaped gardens riotous with summer flowers. At the top of a gently rising lawn sat an impressive period mansion with ornate twisty chimneys and gabled upper windows.

'Wow!' said Jean. 'He must be a millionaire.'

There were already a number of cars on the gravelled square in front of a row of outhouses, and other cars had followed them in.

'I thought it was only going to be us,' Camilla said, 'but it looks as if there's a real crowd here.'

When Ross had parked they went up wide stone steps to the pillared front porch, where the door stood open. The gracious reception hall was crowded with people. Mr Bolton came forward to greet the newcomers. His foot was still plastered, but he was walking well with the aid of his stick.

'So you found us,' he beamed. 'How nice to see you. So glad you could come. Do make yourselves at home. Have some champagne.' He beckoned to a waiter with a tray, who came to serve them.

Mrs Bolton also came forward to make them welcome. 'The pool and the garden are through the sun lounge,' she pointed. 'You'll find your way around, I expect. Go where you like. We won't be eating just yet. Most people like to swim first.'

Mingling with the crowd, they came across Ken and Lucy talking to the new anaesthetist Bob Bannister, looking very correct with a collar and college tie under his navy blazer.

'It's very grand, isn't it?' Camilla said, gazing at Grinling Gibbons carving on the staircase and round the huge open fireplace.

'You haven't seen anything yet,' said Lucy. 'The swimming pool's fantastic and there's a Spanish-style patio with super changing rooms and showers.'

Glancing up at decorative plaster-work on the lofty ceiling, Camilla caught sight of Dominic Bolton at the top of the broad, curving stairway. Black-haired, suave and handsome, he wore white trousers and an open-necked sports shirt with a silk scarf knotted at his throat. Spotting the hospital group, he waved a hand and came skimming down the stairs to join them.

'Good to see you,' he said, reaching for Camilla's hand and pressing it warmly. He then shook hands with Jean and Ross and was introduced to those he had not met.

'I thought you were based in Paris,' Camilla said. 'Have you come over specially?'

'I've finished there now. I was on a course at the Sorbonne.'

'Oh? What are you studying?'

'I'm going to concentrate on portrait painting.'

A svelte blonde in a clinging scarlet dress with a plunging neckline joined them, tucking her arm through Dominic's. 'Darling, you mustn't keep all these nice people to yourself,' she cooed. 'Introduce me.'

'Hallo, Michaela,' Dominic sounded rather bored. 'These nice people looked after my father when he was injured. They're all from St Martin's Hospital.'

'I know one of them already,' she said, glancing at Ross in a coquettish manner. 'Hallo, Ross darling. Long time no see. This is the last place I expected to find you.'

The registrar's lips smiled but his look was cool. 'How are you?' he returned.

Camilla glanced curiously from one to the other. She gathered by his distant manner that Ross was not overjoyed to see Michaela, whatever their previous acquaintance.

The conversation became more general and presently Dominic said, 'Well, who's for a dip?' His enquiring eyes lingered on Camilla. 'Will you join me?'

'Yes, love to.' She turned to Ross. 'We left our things in the car. Could you unlock it for me, please?'

'Bring mine too, will you?' said Jean.

Camilla followed him out of the house. 'Dominic's rather nice, isn't he?'

'The admiration seems to be mutual. He'll be asking you up to see his etchings next,' Ross growled.

She laughed. 'I wonder if he's got talent?'

'I can imagine it won't take you long to find out!'

'That was a surprise, meeting someone you knew, wasn't it?' she said, peaceably, determined not to be goaded into a heated rejoinder.

'You can say *that* again.'

'I didn't think you were too carried away. You had on your disapproving look.'

A satirical smile flickered across his face. 'Are you an expert on my facial expressions?'

'*That* one I've come to know quite well.'

Saying nothing more, they collected the swimming gear and went back into the house. Most people had by now migrated through the sun lounge and into the garden beyond.

The pool was every bit as inviting as Lucy had described, its blue-tiled surfaces reflecting in the sun-dappled water. Away behind it, broken by rose-beds and herbaceous borders, smooth green lawns sloped down to the willow-lined river. The cool, paved loggia in front of the changing rooms was ornamented with tubs of brilliant blue agapanthus lilies, which lent an exotic air to the scene.

After pausing to admire the view, Camilla went off with the other girls to the ladies' dressing rooms. Michaela, in a miniscule white bikini, ran past them on her way out, her long fair hair tied back in a pony-tail.

By the time they emerged in their swimsuits, Michaela was already in the pool and indulging in some horseplay with Ross. Laughingly she splashed him, whereupon he put a large hand on her head and pushed her under the water. A mischievous grin on his face, he supported her as she came up, gasping. Watching the girl twine her arms around his neck, a shaft of annoyance shot through Camilla. She dived off the springboard, swam the length of the pool and paused for breath at the far side.

Dominic came to join her as she rested, shaking the water from her face. 'You'll have to keep an eye on your girlfriend,' she said, seeing Michaela still flaunting herself at Ross. 'You'll be losing her.'

'Does it worry you?' he asked softly, his eyes following hers.

'Of course not. He's nothing to me. Just a colleague.' She flung herself back on the water, moving her hands and feet gently, enjoying the sensation of floating. The sun becoming too bright for her eyes, she swam back to the side to rest.

Dominic, out of the water, said, 'Come and sit on the grass and tell me the story of your life.' Stooping down, he stretched out a hand to help her up.

They lay side by side in the sunshine. 'Your life's probably been far more interesting than mine. Tell me about Paris . . . I've never been there,' Camilla said.

He turned over on to his stomach, propped himself on one elbow and looked down at her. 'Come with me next weekend and I'll show you.'

She smiled. 'Do you always work this fast?'

'Yes. Well?'

'Sorry. Attractive though it sounds, I shan't be free.'

'You must let me know when you are.'

'I think I shall burn if I stay here much longer with nothing on.' Sitting up, Camilla felt her shoulders. 'I can't take too much sun.'

Admiringly he fingered one of her wet red curls. 'You're a natural redhead. I thought so, by your skin tones. Well, put some clothes on and we'll take a walk down by the river.'

In the ladies' room Lucy and Jean were also towelling themselves dry and getting dressed. 'St Martin's is going to pall after this taste of the high life,' Jean said.

Camilla agreed, stripping off her bikini and carefully patting the tender bits of herself with a towel. There was a vague irritation under her left breast where her bra top had been rubbing. She felt the place and something moved about under her fingers. With a puzzled frown she went to examine it in the mirror.

'What's that?' Lucy asked.

'It's a lump, I think. I've never noticed it before. It doesn't hurt. What do you reckon?'

Lucy came and felt the lump, her expression non-committal. 'Mmm. Looks like an innocent papilloma. But perhaps you should have it properly seen. Pop into my Outpatients' clinic tomorrow and we'll do something about it.' She smiled at Camilla's startled face. 'Don't worry. These things are fairly common, aren't they?'

Rather uncertainly, Camilla smiled back. She finished getting changed and went out with the others to enjoy the rest of the day.

There had been activity in the barbecue area while they were dressing. Aromatic smells floated on the air and meat sizzled over heated burners. A waiter served iced drinks from an alfresco bar.

'I didn't realise I was so hungry,' Camilla said, her mouth watering.

'Me too. What a spread!' added Jean.

A tall-hatted chef served them with juicy steaks and they helped themselves from the large selection of salads before joining the rest of their party at one of the picnic tables.

The men had not yet bothered to change, merely slipping sports shirts over their swimming briefs. Ross's muscled thighs and broad chest gleamed with small golden hairs. Michaela had seated herself beside him, her own bronzed limbs naked beneath her short, towelling robe. Ross treated her with a certain amused tolerance.

Camilla decided she did not approve of Michaela. She turned her own attention to Bob Bannister, who had not been in the pool. 'Don't you like swimming?' she asked.

'Not particularly. I'm not much of a sportsman, but I've enjoyed watching you all. I feel rather a dull person beside these muscle-men.' His owlish gaze wandered towards Ross's athletic thighs.

She laughed. 'It takes more than muscle to make a person interesting. What do you do in your spare time?'

'I fish.'

'Oh, so you probably get on fine with Professor Purbright. My friend Marie says that's his favourite topic of conversation.'

Bob raised a whimsical eyebrow. 'Yes, I've gathered that, although we haven't actually gone into a huddle over it yet.'

Desserts were served. Strawberries with whipped cream, orange and lemon sorbet, delicious charlotte russe. Mr and Mrs Bolton moved among their guests having a friendly word here and there, making sure everyone had enough to eat.

Dominic, once more elegantly attired in white, came to seek out Camilla as she finished her wine. 'I said I'd show you the river.' He held out a hand. 'Let's walk down there while they clear this lot away for the dancing.'

Ross's keen eyes followed their progress as they strolled down the long grassy slope to the willow-fringed water.

In the private boathouse there was a small dinghy with an outboard motor. 'That yours?' Camilla said.

'Yes. I'd like to have taken you out, but sadly the motor's fouled up.'

She lowered herself on to the grass. 'Oh well, this is almost as good.' She hugged her knees, watching the craft which plied up and down the river and pointing out colourful dragonflies which hovered over a clumb of yellow water irises.

Dominic watched Camilla. He studied her with an artist's eye. 'You've got an interesting face,' he said.

'All faces are interesting in some way, aren't they?'

'Some more than others. Yours is compulsive viewing. Extraordinary alive. I bet you've got a mind of your own, haven't you?'

She grinned at him. 'That's a polite way of

putting it. I have been called stubborn, among other things.'

'I'd love to paint you. Will you sit for me?'

'I don't think I'd have the time, or the patience. Are you a modern? Do you paint people with one eye in the middle of their foreheads?'

'No. I'm quite square. I put all the features in the right places. Come up to my studio now and I'll show you some of my work.'

Remembering Ross's scathing comment, Camilla laughed softly. He helped her up off the grass. 'Did I say something funny?'

'Not really. It was just a private thought.'

His studio was at the top of the house, an airy room with large windows all round to let in maximum light. There was a strong smell of paint and turpentine and a collection of canvasses, some completed, others half-finished. Her eyes focused on one striking portrait of a blonde girl in a riding habit. The brown eyes followed one everywhere.

'That's Michaela, isn't it?' she said.

'Yes.'

'Are you and she . . . ?'

'Michaela flits from flower to flower like the proverbial honey-bee. She tells me she was engaged to our friend Ross Noble once.' He pushed Camilla gently back on to a stool and moved the neckline of her sun-top to bare her shoulders. 'Just sit there while I make a quick sketch of you.'

Picking up a sketch pad, he drew deftly for some

minutes. Her nose began to tickle and she rubbed it.

'Stop fidgeting,' he ordered.

'I want to sneeze. It's the paint.'

'Okay, I've more or less finished now.'

She let the sneeze come and went to have a look at his work. 'Oh, that's quite good. Are you going to give it to me?'

'Certainly not. I want it for myself.' He put the pad down and laid his hands on her bare shoulders, gazing into her eyes teasingly. 'You do things to my equilibrium. If I kissed you, would you object?'

She laughed. 'No. Thanks for even bothering to ask.'

He gathered her into a close embrace and kissed her long and ardently. It was a pleasurable feeling, knowing that she was desirable, but other than that the kiss in no way moved her.

Sounds of music were filtering up from the garden. Gently she disengaged herself. 'I think it's time we rejoined the party, don't you?'

Dominic sighed. 'I'd rather stay here. But if that's what you'd rather do . . .'

'Yes, I'd like to dance,' she said.

'Okay, you win.'

Dancing was already in full swing when they returned to the garden. Taking her into his arms, Dominic nestled his cheek against her hair while they swayed to the music. Coloured lights twinkling among the surrounding trees lent a romantic air to the scene. Camilla, seeing Ross dancing with

Michaela, gave the pair of them a long, pensive look. She wondered whether this was the great reconciliation. She supposed she should feel glad for him, but she couldn't.

With a firm resolve, she turned her attention back to Dominic who was telling her about an exhibition he was planning at a London gallery. 'You must come and see it,' he said. 'I'll let you know when.'

She danced also with Ken and with Bob, but mostly with Dominic. Ross did not ask her. In fact he and Michaela sat out much of the time, talking together.

The evening sky blazed with the glory of the setting sun and presently, like a ball of fire, it slipped down behind the darkening woods. The band played their last number. Guests began to leave and a reluctant Dominic kissed Camilla good-bye. 'You could stay on and let me run you back later,' he suggested hopefully.

'No, I'd better not, thanks all the same,' she said. 'I'm working tomorrow.'

After expressing their thanks to the Boltons, the hospital group made for their respective cars. Lucy waved as they set off. 'Bye. See you tomorrow, Camilla. I'll look out for you.'

Camilla had momentarily pushed aside the dis-covery of her breast lump and the reminder stirred the small seed of worry at the back of her brain.

The journey back to London passed quickly as they discussed the events of the day. There were odd flashes of summer lightning in the darkening sky and a distant rumble of thunder. Arriving first at Jean's flat, she made them coffee before Ross took Camilla on home.

'Where did you disappear to with the prodigal son this afternoon?' he asked abruptly.

She grinned. 'He took me to see his etchings, like you said he would. He's pretty good, too.'

'At what?'

'At his work. He did a lightning sketch of me. It was great.'

Ross was unimpressed. 'A playboy with a minimum of talent, no doubt,' he scoffed.

'That's a grudging attitude. Why do you dislike him?'

'I dislike all he stands for.'

'That doesn't seem to apply to his friend Michaela. You didn't exactly give *her* the cold shoulder, I noticed,' Camilla retorted.

'I'm amazed you were aware of anyone else with the attentions our artistic friend was paying you.'

'Oh dear,' she sighed. 'Don't be all disapproving again. It's been such a lovely day.'

Unexpectedly he said, 'Oh, pay no attention. Michaela has that effect upon me.'

She stole a glance at his disgruntled face. 'Why? Because you're still in love with her?'

'How do you know I ever was?'

'Dominic said she told him you were once engaged.'

He pursed his lips. 'That was a long time ago, and the ashes are dead.'

'But . . . she was the chip on your shoulder?'

'She gave me problems once,' he admitted. 'I'm glad I saw her today. It was cleansing to know she was completely out of my system.'

Camilla felt unreasonably cheered. 'If it improves your temper, Alleluia!'

He pulled the car to a standstill outside the flat and turned his gaze upon her. 'Have I been that impossible?'

'Sometimes. To me, at any rate.'

She felt her colour rise as their eyes met. Emotion caught at her throat. She swallowed nervously, wanting him to take her in his arms, wanting him to want her.

She had been so jealous of Michaela. *Oh Ross! I could really love you*, she thought with a kind of desperation. But because he was over his old love did not mean he was ready for a new one. In any case, he had said he was finished with women. It was a futile exercise to let herself fall for someone who was determined to go it alone.

'Well, thanks for the lift Ross, good night,' she said, putting on a bright smile.

'Good night, Camilla.' He took the hand she offered and lifted it casually to his lips.

It was nothing more than that, but it threw her completely. His warm lips on her flesh set her heart pounding. She hardly noticed large splashes of rain as she got out of the car. Climbing the stairs to the flat her legs felt totally inadequate.

Enervated from her day in the sun, her cheeks even pinker after Ross's uncharacteristic gesture, Camilla trailed into the living-room.

Marie was still up and watching the midnight movie. It was just finishing and she switched off the set. 'Hi! Had a good day? What was it like?'

'Super.' Camilla flopped into a chair and gave an enthusiastic account of the happenings at Mulberry Court. 'Ross Noble's ex-girlfriend happened to be there too,' she concluded. 'She was quite stunning, actually. I think she would have liked to kiss and make up. She was all over him, but he wasn't having any.' She yawned. 'Fresh air is so exhausting, isn't it? I'm going to bed.'

In the kitchen Camilla rinsed out her bikini and hung it on the overhead airer before going to her room. Undressing, she remembered again the small lump under her breast and the nagging unease returned. She went to show it to Marie in the bathroom.

'Mmm. You ought to get that looked at,' Marie said, raising an eyebrow.

'Lucy's going to see me in Outpatients tomorrow.'

'Oh, that's good. It's useful having friends in the business.'

Except that it wouldn't make any difference to the end result, Camilla thought despondently. The rain had come on in earnest, lashing against her bedroom window. Vivid lightning lit the sky as she went to draw the curtains. It was followed by an earth-shaking roll of thunder and another vivid flash.

Marie came running in looking petrified. Storms were the one thing that were guaranteed to put her in a flap. 'It's right overhead!' she said in a scared voice. 'Can I come in with you?'

Camilla laughed. 'Come on, let's go and make a cup of tea. We shan't sleep with this racket going on.'

In half an hour the storm had passed on, but it was a long time before Camilla could settle down to sleep. She was filled with a sense of foreboding. It seemed as though the storm personified the disaster that could be about to overtake her.

CHAPTER EIGHT

CAMILLA set off for work early the following morning. Only a few puddles remained in the gutters as evidence of the previous night's turbulence. The air smelled fresh and invigorating, but it did little to allay her mounting fears about her consultation with Lucy.

Discharges and admissions since her days off had resulted in many new faces on Simpson Ward. She threw herself wholeheartedly into the job of getting to know them. Familiarising herself with their problems kept her well occupied for most of the morning. Twelve o'clock came before she knew it.

The patients' lunches had arrived when Jean Hunter sought her out. 'Camilla, I thought you were meant to be going down to see Lucy this morning, about that lump?'

'Oh yes,' Camilla gave a nervous laugh. 'I was, wasn't I? Shall I just help with the lunches first?'

'No. You go now and get it over with. You're only putting it off.'

'All right.' With a resigned sigh, Camilla washed her hands and with vague misgivings took the lift down to Outpatients. She approached the SEN in charge of Lucy's clinic, the morning session of which was now practically at an end.

'Doctor Greene's expecting me, if you wouldn't mind telling her I'm here.'

'Okay, her last patient's in there now.' The nurse, a married part-timer, smiled at Camilla and stayed talking with her until the patient came out.

'Staff Nurse Clifton to see you, Doctor,' she said, putting her head round the door.

'Oh, fine. Send her in. Hallo, Camilla,' Lucy said brightly, looking up from the notes she was making on the last case. 'Right.' She put the file aside. 'Just undo the top of your uniform and slip off your bra. Let's have a proper look at this thing.'

Camilla did as requested. 'Nothing much, is it?' she asked, trying to sound unconcerned.

Lucy felt around. 'We-ell,' she said guardedly, 'one shouldn't ignore these things. Cover yourself up a minute . . .' She went through the communicating door to another office, returning in a few moments followed by the powerful figure of Ross.

Camilla blushed to the roots of her hair. *Oh God! Not you*, she thought, instinctively holding her dress together.

'I hear you've got a problem?' He gave her a straight glance, his manner down to earth and professional. Pulling up a chair, he sat down in front of her. 'Let me see.'

Her throat dried, but accepting the inevitable, she bared her chest again and submitted to his sensitive fingers expertly exploring her roundness. He located the small moveable mass on the undersurface of her breast. She was embarrassingly aware of the visible thump of her heart as it bounded against her chest wall.

'When did you first notice this?'

'Well, not really till yesterday. It doesn't hurt.'

'Any family history of this sort of thing?'

She shook her head. 'I don't think so.'

'Mmmm. Well, we'd better investigate it. How are we fixed, Lucy? Someone cancelled for Wednesday's list, didn't they? We could take Camilla in tomorrow.'

'Wh-why the hurry?' Camilla faltered, her pulse stampeding.

'No time like the present, since we've got the bed.'

'And . . . wh-what will you do?'

'Remove the lump, of course, and do a biopsy while you're still under,' explained Ross patiently. 'You know the drill.'

She broke into stormy tears and buried her face in her hands. 'I won't have my breast off! I won't! I won't!'

'Now listen to me, you silly girl.' His voice was stern, but his eyes were compassionate as he pulled her hands away from her face and held them tightly in his. 'You know as well as I do that we only do radical mastectomies when all else fails. Certainly not for something like this. If there were the slightest suspicion of anything sinister I'd remove the axillary glands, but that's all. I agree with Lucy, it looks like an innocent new growth, but we have to make sure. All right now?'

She gulped back a sob, wiped her hand across her eyes and nodded reluctantly.

'In any case,' he went on, 'even if we found anything, the success rate for breast tumours is good when taken early. Chin up.' He turned to Lucy. 'Get her to sign the consent form now and then she can arrange to go sick for a few days.' He went back to his own office.

Camilla found a tissue and blew her nose, making an effort to get a grip on herself as more tears threatened.

'He's right, you know,' Lucy said with a sympathetic smile. 'The sooner you have something done, the better. Will you ring up your family?'

'Oh no. I—I'll w-wait until . . . there's something p-positive to tell them.'

'Maybe you're right,' Lucy agreed. 'No sense in alarming them unnecessarily. Well, let's get on with the necessary.' She set about taking a blood test and listening to Camilla's lungs, after which she wrote out a request for a chest X-ray. 'There you are, get this done and we'll see you on the ward tomorrow.'

'Well,' Jean asked when Camilla returned, 'how did it go?'

'They want me to come in tomorrow. Ross is going to do a biopsy.' She had got over her initial shock by now and her voice sounded comparatively normal.

Jean nodded approval. 'I thought they might. Would you like to go off? I'll let the nursing officer know.'

Camilla gave a quick shake of her head. 'For goodness' sake, Jean, I'm not ill. I'd rather stay and work. It'll give me less time to think about it.'

'All right. It's up to you. I should take your lunch-break now then.'

Down in the canteen, Camilla was glad to meet up with Marie at the counter. Having been served with toasted sandwiches and coffee, they found a table on their own.

'You seen Lucy?' Marie asked, eyeing her observantly.

'Yes. She got Ross to examine me. They're whipping me in tomorrow.' Her voice quavered. 'I made a fool of myself, Marie. I howled in front of him.'

Marie made sympathetic noises. 'Oh well, I'm sure he understood.'

'I felt such an idiot.'

'You wouldn't be the first to react like that. Anyway, it may prove to be nothing very dreadful, so try not to look on the black side.'

Camilla gave a wan smile. She felt as if there were a question mark hanging over the whole of the rest of her life. How could she not be anxious?

June and Yvonne came to join them at their table.

'You both look very sober,' said June. 'What's up?'

Marie explained and the other girls commiserated.

'Well, I vote we all go down to The Friars

tonight,' put in Yvonne supportively. 'No sense in staying home and getting worked up about it. Come and drown your sorrows.'

For Camilla the rest of the day passed in an atmosphere of unreality. During the afternoon she saw the nursing officer who said she was not to worry and that she would arrange for an agency nurse to take Camilla's place. Back at the flat at five o'clock, she shampooed her hair, packed a weekend bag with the things she would need, tidied her bedroom and did some washing. Anything to stop her reliving that scene with Ross. She felt ashamed of herself for giving way. It wasn't going to be easy to face him again after her outburst, but if it came to the worst she was determined to behave with more dignity.

Marie made a trip to the local take-away for their evening meal, after which they joined the other two girls at The Friars for the suggested cheer-up sessions. Both Marie and Yvonne were to be in Theatre when Camilla was due for surgery.

'We'll make sure they don't cut the wrong bit out,' joked Yvonne before they parted company.

It felt peculiar to Camilla being a patient in Simpson's side ward the following afternoon, and being at the receiving end of routines she normally carried out on other people. However, the staff left her little time for brooding. Jean and various other people on the ward flitted in and out for this or that reason and whenever they had a free moment. Lucy came to talk and Bob Bannister came to put her through his pre-anaesthesia checks.

'You'll do,' he said, replacing his stethoscope in his pocket and giving her a benign smile. 'I'll see you downstairs in the morning.'

Camilla wondered nervously whether Ross would come and was rather relieved when he did not. That he had been on the ward, she knew. Perhaps he'd decided it best not to risk a repetition of a show of hysterics, she thought.

Before going off duty, Jean popped in to say good night. 'They're slipping you in first thing in the morning,' she said, 'so you won't have long to wait. Ross has ordered you a sedative so that you don't lie awake worrying. I've told the night staff.'

With the aid of the tablets Camilla did sleep well, and only awoke when the night staff nurse came to do her routine observations.

'No tea for you this morning,' she said breezily. 'You're down for eight-thirty. If you'd like to have your bath now we can get you gowned up and give you your pre-med.'

Now that the well-known ritual had begun, Camilla felt quite resigned. She put on dressing-gown and slippers and went along to the bathroom. When she returned the operating gown was on her bed. She exchanged her nightdress for the shapeless garment, got between the sheets and surrendered her fate to destiny.

By the time the theatre porters came for her, the pre-medication had taken over and she was relaxed and drowsy. Transferring her from bed to trolley, one of the men exclaimed, 'Cor! Wish they was all featherweights like you.'

Camilla gave a sleepy grin. 'I'll be lighter still when I come back,' she murmured.

Matty went along with her, making inconsequential small talk on the way, handing her over at the anaesthetics room with the words, 'Good luck, Cam.'

A couple of the theatre staff gathered around her, friendly eyes peering over their masks. She felt like a laboratory specimen. Briefly she recognised Yvonne and Lucy and glimpsed Ross's large frame hovering in the distance. Then there was Bob taking her hand and selecting a suitable vein. 'Right. They're ready for you now. Here we go, Camilla.'

She watched him insert the needle into the back of her hand . . . saw him push the plunger of the syringe . . . and that was all.

Jean Hunter's voice seemed to come from a long way off. 'Hallo, Camilla. You're back on the ward.'

She struggled to push through the fog in her brain. The room swam mistily for a moment before her eyes focused first on the dark blue uniform and then on Jean's serene face bending over her. It took her time to recall where she was and why. Her left arm was lying on a pillow . . . and there was a nagging hurt in the region of her breast. The reason crystallised. She put her hand to the place and found the dressing. Then her fingers explored her armpit. It was intact; nothing had been done there. Wide-eyed now, she looked at Jean. 'I—it wasn't . . . ?'

'No,' said Jean with a glad smile, 'it wasn't. Just a benign adenoma.'

'Oh God!' Camilla gave an enormous sigh. 'Aren't I lucky?' she said in a weak voice.

'Yes, aren't you. Come on, let's raise you up a bit.' Jean plumped up a pillow and put it in position. 'Not hurting too much?' Camilla shook her head. 'Good. Go back to sleep for a while and we'll tidy you up later.'

It was no effort to drift back into peaceful oblivion, but presently the soreness and discomfort of the surgical incision woke her properly. She lay there quietly putting up with the throb, overwhelmed to find her fears unfounded, grateful to everyone for their concern.

Matty came in. 'Hallo, mate,' she said blithely. 'How are you feeling?'

'A bit battered, but otherwise wonderful,' Camilla said with a limp smile.

'Yes, great news, isn't it? We're all chuffed. Got to do your obs.' Matty took the thermometer from its holder, shook it down and popped it under Camilla's tongue. 'We'll wash you and get you out of this passion-killer in a minute,' she said, in between checking pulse and respirations.

'Thanks.' Camilla raised another smile although in fact she was feeling none too brilliant. Her throat was dry, her head woolly and her breast throbbed persistently.

After charting her observations Matty brought a

bowl of warm washing water on a trolley and manoeuvred the bed into a sitting position. Then she found Camilla's toilet things and helped her to wash.

Camilla was amazed how frail she felt with the effort of merely washing her face and hands and cleaning her teeth. Finally, with Matty's help, she put on her own Swiss cotton nightie and sank back against the pillows. 'Gosh! I feel exhausted.'

'Yes, a general anaesthetic takes it out of you. You're written up for some Omnopon. I'll get it. And would you like a cup of tea?'

'Please. I can wait though, if you're busy.'

'Stop trying to be a model patient,' grinned Matty, bustling out with the washing trolley. 'You lie there like Lady Muck and enjoy yourself while you've got the chance.'

Her aches and pains subsided as the injection took over. It was heavenly just to lie there, knowing her worry had been groundless and not having to bother about anything. Images floated through her consciousness. This was the room Fern Debden had been in. Camilla had little realised that she herself would soon be occupying the same bed. She wondered if Fern had noticed that the blue flowers on the cream chintzy bed curtains made a pattern like noughts and crosses?

The curtains were different in other wards. Her mind wandered to ITU where they were a restful apple green. It brought back thoughts of Julian. Poor Julian . . . a promising life nipped in the bud. But in the circumstances perhaps it was as well he had gone when he did; better than a living death with brain damage.

She thought about the barbecue and of Ross and Michaela, and of how relationships could sour peoples' lives. And she remembered again with regret her own loss of control when Ross had said she must come in for surgery. As Marie had remarked, he was probably used to people panicking when faced with the unknown, but all the same, she wished she hadn't let herself down.

It was five o'clock when Marie came bounding in with a bunch of freesias. 'Hi, Cam! How're you doing? You look great.'

Camilla smiled. 'I feel great. It's marvellous, being let off the hook.'

'I know. When the result of the biopsy came through we all cheered. Think they'd have cracked a bottle of champagne in Theatre if there'd been one handy. Anything I can get you?'

'No, thanks. I shouldn't be here long, once I get my sea-legs. There's no drain to come out.' She picked up the flowers and sniffed them. 'Mmmm . . . thanks for these.'

'I'll get something to put them in . . . they're pretty busy in the ward, what with the other cases.' She disappeared to the kitchen and came back with a suitable vase.

'Oh, Marie, it's your birthday tomorrow,' Camilla remembered, 'and I haven't even got you a card. This business put it right out of my head.'

'Never mind about that. We'll have a dinner

party when you're up and about . . . make it a sort of double celebration.'

Ross came to see her later that night. 'Well?' he said, mildly, casting his discerning eyes over her. 'Happier now?'

She blushed. 'Yes, thank you.' To her dismay she felt her chin wobble and her eyes brim with tears.

'Hey!' he said softly, sitting down on the bed and stroking her cheek with the back of his hand. 'There's nothing to cry about. You should be laughing.'

'I know.' She dabbed her eyes with a corner of the sheet. 'I-it's just the relief. And I'm sorry I got a bit hysterical the other day . . .'

He gave a slight smile. 'Understandable in the circumstances.'

'I-it *was* benign . . . you are sure? I mean . . . there's no doubt?'

'Camilla!' He looked at her under his straight brows. 'I'd be ordering you chemotherapy if it weren't, wouldn't I?'

'Sorry,' she said hastily, 'Only . . . it's almost too good to be true.'

'It's been a difficult time for you, especially . . . on top of Julian's accident.'

With his probing eyes upon her she felt she had to put the record straight. 'Of course, I was terribly sad about Julian. But I wasn't in love with him. There was nothing like that between us.'

'Oh! I see.' He paused before he went on briskly, 'Well, that's something at any rate. I shouldn't like to think of your life being shattered. Will you go home to Dorset when I let you out of here?'

'Depends how much time you give me.'

'I should prefer you to stick around until your stitches come out. After that we'll let you convalesce for a week. Will you feel like driving yourself?'

'Oh yes, I'll be fine.'

'Right. I'll see you again.' With a brief nod he left her.

Gazing after his departing figure, Camilla felt a sense of peace. They had actually talked agreeably. There had been no undercurrent of tension between them. It was lovely to be on reasonable terms with him, even if that was all it would ever amount to.

It was her mother who answered the telephone when, feeling more like herself the next day, Camilla rang to put them in the picture.

'Oh dear!' Mrs Clifton said with a show of concern. 'You should have let us know. People must think your family are an uncaring lot, not to have enquired about you.'

'No they don't, Mummy. They knew it was my decision not to say anything until we knew the result. And fortunately I'm okay.'

'Well, that's a blessing, isn't it? And you say you'll be home for a few days . . . when will that be?'

'Probably about Monday.'

'Oh bother!' Her mother clicked her tongue. 'Isn't it always the way! We shan't be here. Your dad and I are going to Bristol this weekend, it's an exchange visit with Father Bisley, the Vicar of St Faith's. We can't very well cancel now. Never mind, dear. Grandma will be here . . . she'll look after you.'

Camilla made an unspectacular recovery, although her breast was quite tender for a while. A few days later Ross inspected it, agreed that the stitches could come out and then she could go.

'Did you ever get that fan belt tightened?' he asked in a businesslike fashion.

'No, but I will do before I go home.'

'I'll come over this evening and fix it for you.'

'Are you sure? I don't like to trouble you . . .'

'It will be time well spent if it gives me peace of mind,' he said wryly.

Jean Hunter's wedding had been fixed for a fortnight hence. 'You've timed things nicely,' she said, chatting with Camilla while they waited for the taxi to take her back to the flat. 'You'll be back here by then and I'd like you to come.'

Saying goodbye to the staff, Camilla was half glad, half sorry to leave. 'You've all been terrific,' she smiled. 'I could get addicted to this kind of treatment.'

True to his word, later that evening Ross arrived at the flat to adjust the fan belt on her car and afterwards came upstairs for a quick coffee with the two girls.

On leaving, he said, 'We shall miss having you around, Camilla. Take care of yourself.'

'You know, I think he really meant that,' observed Marie. 'He wasn't joking.'

Camilla didn't comment, but her mind played out a fantasy of Ross actually looking forward to her return, his face lighting up at the sight of her. Then she brought herself sharply back to earth. It was pathetic to lapse into pipe-dreams just because he had paid her a slight compliment. It was probably only said in fun anyway.

The next day she arrived at the vicarage in Christchurch to be greeted by a loving hug from her grandmother and a string of questions as to whether everything was really all right.

'Your mother felt quite guilty,' she said, 'to think you'd gone through all that without letting anyone know.'

'Oh, I've lots of good friends at the hospital,' Camilla explained. 'It wasn't as if I was among strangers.'

'Well, we shall make a fuss of you while you are here. Father Bisley and his wife are out at the moment . . . they're a very nice couple you'll find; they don't stand on ceremony. Anyway, their being here won't interfere with anything you want to do.'

'Oh, I'm quite happy just to hang around for a bit. Shall we have a day's shopping in Bournemouth? I have to buy a birthday present for Marie, also a wedding present and something to wear.'

Camilla told her grandmother about Jean's forthcoming wedding. 'I've never been to one in the hospital chapel before. It should be lovely.'

The visiting minister and his wife proved to be a middle-aged, homely pair, who treated Camilla with a great show of warmth and interest.

'So you're on sick leave, my dear?' said Mrs Bisley with motherly concern. 'Don't let our being here put any strain on you. You do exactly as you want. We can find plenty to do, and your father's nice curate is being very helpful.'

Stephen came round that evening, delighted to find her there. He cornered her in the hall when she came down from unpacking. 'Now you are sure you're all right?' he said, anxious brown eyes searching her face.

'Yes, perfectly, Stephen,' she laughed. 'I feel a bit of a fraud really.'

'Fraud or not, I shall take you under my wing. In loco parentis, so to speak.' Again he put forward the desirability of taking life at a slower pace. 'Too much stress in the Big Smoke. I don't know how you can tolerate it.'

She laughed. 'I thrive on it. A few days down here and I'll be itching to get back again.'

And it was true. The miles which separated her from St Martin's, but more especially from Ross Noble, yawned like a vast impenetrable chasm. Just to be near him had become an indispensable element of her existence. Without him she felt aimless, as though life itself was leading nowhere.

'Well, it's my day off tomorrow,' Stephen went on. 'Will you spend it with me?'

'Yes, that would be nice. What shall we do?'

'Take a picnic into the country. I'll see to it.'

The next morning he picked her up in his lovingly-tended veteran runabout and they set off towards Ringwood in the New Forest, ending up at a picnic spot by the Avon where they watched fishermen casting their lines into the fertile waters. They saw the sapphire flash of a kingfisher as it dived for a minnow, and the shimmer of steel-blue wings as swallows wheeled and soared. Camilla lay back, idly chewing on a piece of grass, soothed by the rural scene although her thoughts were miles away.

'I wish you'd let me look after you,' Stephen said presently, his brown eyes solicitous.

She smiled. 'I don't need looking after.'

'Yes, you do. Camilla, marry me.' He stopped her when she would have interrupted. 'Yes, I know you don't think about me like that. But marriage isn't all sex. It's the uniting of two minds as well as bodies. We have the same background . . . I believe we think along the same lines. And no one could love you more than I do. Don't you think that's a good start? That you might grow to love me . . . ?'

In the face of his arguments she felt wretched at having to hurt him. 'I'm sorry, Steve, really I am. Don't pressure me. I do like you very much, you know that. But maybe I'm not ready for marriage, yet, to anyone.'

He shrugged, and lightly ruffled her hair. 'All right. Time will tell.' They let the matter drop.

She had an enjoyable shopping session with her grandmother the following day. For Marie she bought a butter-dish in the Denbyware she was collecting. For Jean's wedding present she chose half a dozen crystal sherry glasses, and for her wedding outfit she decided on a coral-pink dress with a white piping trim. She found a little white beribboned boater to sit on the back of her glowing hair.

'You look pretty enough to be a bridesmaid,' her grandmother said.

The rest of her stay passed quickly. The visiting minister and his wife were easy to get along with and Camilla was well-used to talking to strangers. But she was glad when it was time for her to go back to London. It felt almost like returning from exile. Stephen waved her off on Friday afternoon, his wistful expression making her regret that she'd agreed to spend the day with him. Perhaps she had been wrong to do that if it had aroused his hopes.

Marie was pleased to see her back that evening and was delighted with her birthday present.

'I've arranged our dinner party for tomorrow, Cam,' she said. 'Luke's going to see to the booze. We can shop in the morning. I thought beef stroganoff, which we can heat at the last minute, and fresh fruit salad and cream for afters, or do you think syllabub?'

'Oh, fruit salad would be fine, I should think. Who's coming?'

Marie ticked off the people on her fingers. 'There'll be you, me, Luke, Ken and Lucy, Bob Bannister and Yvonne. And I asked Ross,' she said with an uncertain glance at Camilla. 'That makes a nice round number . . . you quite like him, don't you?'

'Mmm,' Camilla said. 'A bit embarrassing though, seeing how he operated on my boob.' Her colour rose at the thought.

'Oh! Come on,' laughed Marie. 'He's seen so many boobs, what's one more or less?'

On Saturday morning they did their shopping and spent the afternoon getting the meal ready. Then they tidied the flat and set the table in readiness. Camilla made a little centrepiece of roses which she had brought from the vicarage garden, and Marie stuck pink candles into the necks of old wine bottles.

By then it was time to bath and change into their party gear.

'Look at me!' crowed Marie, coming into Camilla's bedroom in a new cherry-red dress. She smoothed her hands over her hips. 'Down to a size twelve at last!'

'Yes, you look great,' said Camilla admiringly. 'What shall I wear? I've got nothing new.'

She finally settled on the striped silk dress she had worn to the Shakespeare play at the Barbican. 'The last time I wore this,' she remembered sadly,

'Julian was alive.'

The doorbell rang then, putting an end to nostalgia. It was Luke arriving with the drinks and they had a pre-party Martini together.

The other guests followed soon afterwards, the last to come being Ross. Camilla ran downstairs to let him in. She felt breathless at the sight of him. His tawny hair further bleached by the sun, his muscled limbs neatly clad in well-fitting leisure trousers and stylish shirt, he looked a powerhouse of virility.

'Hallo! How are you?'

The deeply resonant voice sent wild longing surging through her veins. 'Fine, thanks,' she returned. 'And you?'

His intensely blue eyes twinkled as he looked her over. 'If you really want to know, I've been suffering from withdrawal symptoms.'

'Well, you don't look too worried about it, so I shan't ask what sort,' she said flippantly, running upstairs ahead of him.

They served fluffy rice and courgettes with the beef and were complimented on their efforts. After the meal, having dumped the dirties in the kitchen, they played a silly card game for pennies and laughed a lot. Later Luke put on some music and furniture was pushed aside for dancing.

'Shall we?' said Ross to Camilla as the other couples paired up. His arms closed about her and her body burned at his touch. He looked down at her with a crooked smile. 'This is a first, isn't it?

You didn't dance with me at the barbecue.'

'You didn't ask me. Besides, if I remember, you were rather busy elsewhere.'

'Ah, yes. But then we both were. Have you seen the pushy painter since then?'

'No. I've hardly had time.'

'I suppose not. And you're back at work on Monday?'

'Yes. Are we full up on Simpson?'

'When are we not? And Jean leaves during the week, I believe, to get ready for her nuptials. Your hair smells nice,' he said irrelevantly.

The record finished and they all changed partners.

It was past midnight before they stopped for coffee and sat around talking. The conversation veered to the forthcoming wedding and Marie and Luke mentioned they had fixed on a date for their own towards the end of the year.

'You'd better watch out, Lucy. This thing could catch on,' Ken said.

Lucy raised her eyebrows mischievously. 'Do you reckon that was a proposal?' she asked the company.

Ross looked at Ken. 'It's a hard life, you know, getting tied up with a medic. Your most intimate moments summarily cut short because someone has a heart attack or whatever.'

'At least being in the business, I should understand, although I might not be too pleased,' said Ken, and he and Lucy exchanged smiles.

'I suppose there's something to be said for going into it with your eyes open,' Ross allowed.

The party eventually broke up and everyone kissed everyone else goodbye. But there was no special significance in Ross's salute to Camilla. In fact it couldn't have been more perfunctory. She felt it was simply a social gesture to be got over as quickly as possible. It certainly had no hint of the fire with which he had kissed her that time at his flat. Which made it clear that she in no way mattered to him, other than as a member of staff. A cloud of desolation descended over her when he had gone.

Marie, Luke and she attacked the washing-up together before, leaving them to their goodbyes, Camilla took herself off to bed.

Sadly she had to admit that simply being friends with Ross was no solution. It left her with an even worse ache inside. At least when they were fighting it gave her some grounds for trying to convince herself that she disliked him. But when he was being well-behaved and agreeable it was impossible to deny that she was not hopelessly in love with the man.

Perhaps, after all, it would be more sensible to leave St Martin's and put the bedevilling Ross Noble out of mind forever. Stephen had said he loved her. Should she settle for that if he were prepared to take the risk? Perhaps, as he'd said, she would grow to love him. She supposed it might sometimes happen that way.

CHAPTER NINE

WHEN CAMILLA had gone to bed that night she had almost convinced herself she would marry Stephen. He was nice, if unexciting. He loved her, and it was a good feeling to know that you mattered that much to someone. But by the morning her thoughts had undergone a change. What an absolutely self-centred idea, to use him as a means of forgetting Ross. Stephen deserved better than that, and he might well meet someone else later who could make him happy.

It also came to her with a kind of relief that there was no need to take the drastic step of marrying anyone in order to get her life together. All she had to do was to settle on the next step in her career. Some of the girls in her set were already making application for post-graduate courses in things like ITU, paediatrics, coronary care, etcetera. Camilla thought she might settle for midwifery; choose an attractive town, perhaps at the seaside. Her living arrangements were going to have to change anyway, with Marie getting married later that year.

She went into work a little easier in her mind for having come to a decision. Not that it was going to help a great deal over the next few months when she would still be faced with almost daily contact with Ross, but at least it would give her an objective.

It was madness to let one person dominate your thoughts to the extent that Ross was dominating hers. Until now she had always been a self-sufficient person. On the whole level-headed, if somewhat impulsive, but quite capable of organising her own life. That affair with Tony Sinclair, for instance, had left her unscathed; and it hadn't ruined her SRN chances as she had feared it might. But that had been just a fun episode. Her feelings for Tony had been nothing compared with the intensity of her feelings for Ross. Well, she would just have to pull herself together and get over him.

The trouble was that whenever their paths crossed her heart lurched and her throat tightened. It became a kind of exquisite torture having to see him and talk to him, even if only about patients. And he was so civil to her now; no longer aggressive as in the past. His attitude towards her seemed to have undergone a change for some reason. She could only assume that he was going easy on her because of her recent health problem. But there was still a certain constraint between them, as though he wished to keep her at arm's length. He behaved more like a polite stranger.

That first week back after her sick leave was a peculiar mixture of events. Camilla had never known the imperturbable Jean to be in such a flap.

'Everything okay for Saturday?' Camilla asked, taking over at midday on Monday.

Jean sighed as she handed over the ward keys. 'I think everything's tied up now. There's been so much to do my brain's gone on strike. I hope it's all plain sailing on the ward for you . . . I've done the off-duty for the next month, and the paperwork's up to date . . .'

She was not due to leave until mid-week and Camilla laughed. 'Good heavens, Jean, you're only going to be away for three weeks. The ward's not going to fall apart. And you've still got till Wednesday . . .'

'Oh, I know. Pre-wedding nerves, I expect. Even Duncan's been a bit uptight lately . . .' She paused to answer the telephone. 'Yes? Yes, we do have a bed—okay.' Replacing the receiver, she went on, 'That was Lucy. They're sending us a Mrs White, head injury and fractured ribs. You'll have to transfer Mrs Lane from High Dependency . . . she's stable now. Can you cope?'

'Yes, of course. There's plenty of us on. You go, and don't worry.'

Gathering up a couple of wedding gifts that had been given to her, Jean departed. The rest of the staff set about moving beds to make room for the new patient. Then there was a flurry of activity with drugs to be given, drips to check, dressings to do and patients to be made comfortable before visitors could be admitted.

Some half-hour later the new patient was brought up on a trolley. Handing Camilla the X-rays and case notes, the Casualty nurse gave her a brief resumé. 'This is Mrs White, she's seventy. Fell off the kitchen steps and was knocked out for a time. Fractured ribs and a left pneumothorax. The registrar said he'd put the chest drain in up here. That's her husband with her, nice old boy.'

Camilla went to welcome the elderly lady and direct the porters to the bed which had been prepared.

'Hallo, Mrs White,' she said. 'You've been in the wars, haven't you?'

Her husband, a tall soldierly man with a pleasant manner, answered for her. 'Yes, she will climb about, you know. I'm always telling her not to, but she's a headstrong lass.' Squeezing his wife's hand, he gave her a loving smile and shook his head despairingly.

This description of his white-haired, solidly-built partner, privately amused Camilla, but she said kindly, 'Well, if you'll just wait here while we get her into bed then you can stay with her until the doctor comes.'

The gash on Mrs White's forehead had already been stitched, but the lung damage caused by her fractured ribs was making her breathing painful and laboured. After settling her as comfortably as she could, Camilla wrote out the necessary charts and recorded her observations. 'The doctor shouldn't be too long,' she consoled, 'then he'll probably be able to do something to make your breathing easier.'

Leaving Mr White to sit with his wife, she went

back to the office to make out a Kardex sheet. Going on to the treatment room she then laid up a dressings trolley with the equipment necessary for draining the air and blood which had collected in Mrs White's pleural cavity.

Afternoon teas were about to be served when Ross appeared on the ward.

'Oh, hallo. There you are. Everything okay?' he said with a remote half smile.

'Fine, thanks.' She forced herself to sound as impersonal as he did, in spite of the butterflies in her throat.

'Is Jean about?' he went on.

'No, she's on a half-day. 'Fraid you'll have to put up with me.'

'Right. I'm going to aspirate Mrs White's chest now. Are you going to help me?'

'Yes. I've got the trolley ready. I haven't told her what it entails. Did you?'

Their eyes met fleetingly before he turned his gaze to where Mr White sat stroking his wife's hair back from her forehead. 'Not exactly. I'll go and have a word with them now.'

She watched him as he strolled, loose-limbed, towards the bedside where he pulled out a chair and sat down to talk in that easy, courteous manner he had with patients. With an involuntary sigh Camilla sought out Avis to help wheel the bed to the treatment room.

'All right, sir,' said Ross, rising as the nurses joined him. 'We'll get on with this little job and your wife will feel a great deal better.'

Camilla smiled at the husband. 'If you'd like to wait in the relatives' room, you can see her again when we've finished.' The transfer completed, she sent Avis to take him a cup of tea.

Ross scrubbed his hands and put on the sterile gloves which had been put ready for him. Camilla moved a bed-table into position and placed a pillow on it. 'There you are, Mrs White, just lean forward and rest on this. That's fine.' She untied the tapes at the back of the examination gown.

'I—is it . . . going to hurt?' Mrs White asked nervously.

'I'm going to give you a local anaesthetic,' Ross reassured her. 'You'll feel a prick, but the rest shouldn't be too uncomfortable.'

After the injection, while they waited for it to take effect he filled the time with cordial conversation. 'They tell me it's their golden wedding anniversary tomorrow,' he remarked, glancing towards Camilla.

'Oh dear!' She gave the patient a sympathetic smile. 'This is a fine way to celebrate it.'

'And the family . . . had planned a party for us . . . on Saturday . . .' wheezed Mrs White.

'Never mind. You'll have to have it later, won't you?' Camilla said.

When he was satisfied that the local anaesthetic had taken effect, Ross carefully introduced the cannula into a selected space between the ribs and withdrew some of the fluid for laboratory testing.

He was very gentle. 'All right, my dear?' he asked.

She was gripping Camilla's hand tightly and nodded.

'Good.' He then connected plastic tubing to the hollow needle to allow continued draining into an underwater-sealed bottle. 'Nearly over now. I'm just going to put a couple of stitches in to keep this tube in place.'

The procedure completed, Ross stripped off his gloves and went to the office to label his samples. Camilla applied a dry dressing around the drain and settled Mrs White comfortably against her pillows before again recording pulse and respirations.

'Okay, Mr White,' she said, going to find him when his wife had been returned to the ward, 'you can go back to her now. But don't stay too long, she needs to be quiet for awhile.'

'All right, my lovely, I won't. I'll just see what things she wants me to bring in. And thanks for all you're doing. You're a smashing lot.'

Still in the office writing up his notes, Ross looked up briefly when Camilla went back to him. 'Fifty years of marriage! Quite an endurance test.'

'That would depend on your partner, I suppose,' she returned. 'They seem a very devoted couple. She is going to be all right, isn't she?'

'Oh yes, I think so. For her age she's a healthy lady. She'll probably have a black eye after that bang on the head, but the concussion appears to be only mild.' He finished his writing and got up to leave, putting his pen away in his top pocket. 'How old are you?'

The question was totally unexpected. 'Twenty-two,' she answered. 'Why?'

'Mmmm. Still time for you to make the half-century.'

She gave a short laugh. 'I'm not aiming to lose my independence for a long time yet.'

'No? Well, time's running out for me. I'm thirty-four today.'

'Oh! Many happy returns. This seems to be a week of celebrations.' She paused. 'I thought marriage didn't figure in your plans anyway?'

He gave a wry smile. 'It's not only women who can change their minds. I've written Mrs White up for hydrocortisone and some cough linctus,' he added, returning to ward matters, and he strode away. She was completely bemused. Perhaps, after seeing Michaela again, the ashes were not so dead as he had thought. That might be great for him but it left her feeling more wretched than ever.

Sorting through the post the following morning Jean said, 'There's one here for you, Camilla.'

'For me?' she studied the unfamiliar hand before opening the envelope. Inside was an impressive gilt-edged card. 'Oh, it's from Dominic Bolton . . . it's his art exhibition on Saturday. Well, I shan't be able to go to that, shall I? I'll be too busy seeing you get well and truly wed.'

Jean raised her eyebrows as she read the card.

'He'd obviously like to see you again. Duncan and I will be away by four, so you would have time to pop in afterwards if you wanted to.'

'I'll see.' Camilla put the card in her bag and thought no more about it.

There was a shoal of greetings cards for Mrs White, far too many for her locker-top, so the remainder the nurses stuck to the wall behind her bed. She was an uncomplaining patient, cheerful in spite of her aches and pains. At visiting time that afternoon her husband brought a bouquet of yellow roses which Camilla arranged for her, tying the satin ribbon bow around the vase.

Other members of their large family also came with floral tributes and there was a devoted little gathering around her bed.

'You know, that old boy still looks as if he adores her,' said Jean with a smile. 'If Duncan can look at me like that after fifty years, I shan't complain.'

'One thing's for sure,' laughed Camilla, 'you won't bring up a family of seven like they did!'

It was also Jean's last day on duty before the great event. Word of her forthcoming marriage had gone around the ward and one of the more mobile patients had organised a collection with which his wife had bought a silver-plated cake slice as a token of the patients' esteem.

'Oh, that is sweet of you all,' Jean said, quite touched by the gesture, and she went round to thank everyone.

As well as individual gifts from personal friends,

senior staff had combined to buy her a Teasmade. It was to be presented that evening by Professor Purbright in the doctors' Mess.

Camilla had not had dealings with Ross since the day she had helped him with Mrs White's chest drain. Now, arriving at the doctors' Mess, she saw him talking with Lucy as they waited for the Professor to put in an appearance. Since they were both by the door it would have seemed odd to walk on by. She smiled brightly, said, 'Hi!' and stayed to chat for a moment.

Lucy, fortunately, was never at a loss for words which lessened, to some extent, the strain Camilla felt at trying to behave naturally. Even so, her heart raced uncontrollably when Ross's hand rested on her shoulder to move her aside when Professor Purbright himself came in, a plump little Yorkshire terrier cradled in his arms.

'Good evening,' said the professor genially. 'Will one of you look after Abigail for me? I couldn't leave her in the car. It's a difficult time for her. She's going to be a mother! Here you are, my dear.' He transferred the furry bundle to Camilla's arms before making his way over to shake hands with Jean.

Abigail licked Camilla under the chin and she giggled. 'I know I've decided to do midwifery . . . but I hope my first case isn't going to be pups!'

Ross looked curious. He was about to speak when someone called for hush.

Professor Purbright began his rambling tribute to

Jean. Getting round to the presentation at last, he made a close inspection of the Teasmade. 'What an interesting contraption.' He paused and scanned his audience with a dry smile. 'I have a first-rate tea-maker at home . . . and, what's more, she never blows a fuse!' Everyone laughed dutifully. He went on, 'But one of these things might not be a bad investment . . . in case she ever decided to go on strike.' Amid more laughter and applause, he shook hands with Jean and wished her well, even going so far as to peck her on the cheek before coming back to collect his precious pet from Camilla.

At the conclusion of the proceedings Jean had a good many gifts to take home and Camilla rallied round to help her pack them up. 'How are you going to manage . . . get a taxi?'

'No, I've got my car here. I managed to wangle a parking space over at the Medical School.'

'Right, I'll carry some for you.' Camilla armed herself with the large carton containing the Teasmade and balanced an electric blender on top. 'Think we'll have to make two journeys.'

'Here, let me take something for you.' Ross appeared at her elbow and relieved Camilla of her load.

'Oh, thanks, then we can do it all in one go,' she said, picking up the remainder of the things.

They walked the short distance to where Jean's car was parked and stowed the presents on the back seat.

Jean gave a happy sigh, her eyes shining. 'Well, that's that. Thanks for your help. See you both in church on Saturday. Pray for a fine day for me.' With a cheery wave she drove off, leaving the two of them together.

'How long will she be away?' Ross queried.

'Only three weeks. In the meantime you're lumbered with Matty and me and other lowly creatures.'

'This sudden humility . . . it doesn't ring true,' he returned, a mocking glint in his eye. 'Tell me, what was that you were saying about doing midwifery?'

'Oh, I've decided it's about time I got on with the next thing.'

'And are you going to do it here?'

'No. As far away from here as possible,' she said, unthinking.

His eyes narrowed, searching her face. 'Why?'

She shrugged, wishing she hadn't let that slip. 'I—I just feel like a change of scene. And Marie will be leaving later in the year.'

Scratching his cheek thoughtfully, he continued to study her for some moments. She flushed and dropped her gaze, feeling as if her mind were being X-rayed, her most secret thoughts laid bare to him. She was trying to conjure up some pretext to get away when he said, 'What are you running from? Or should I say who?'

Her flush deepened. Had he really read her mind? 'Wh-why should you think that? It's a logical step, isn't it?'

He pursed his lips. 'Just a hunch,' he murmured, and glanced at his wristwatch. 'I'd like to stay and talk about it, but unfortunately I haven't the time right now.'

'Well, don't let me hold you up, and there's nothing to talk about that would concern you,' Camilla said, affecting nonchalance.

'Good night, then.' Giving her a heady smile he turned in the direction of the hospital.

She made her way across the square towards the main gates, utterly forlorn. So much for her good resolution about forgetting him. How could she bear to leave St Martin's when just to hear his voice sent tingles down her spine and to have him smile at her like that filled her with wild longing? Her will-power, her whole world, went topsy-turvy when she was in his company. If she went away she would languish like a plant without sunlight. She hadn't realised what it was like to be so totally captivated by one person. She thought that's what it must have been like for Mr and Mrs White, the way they looked at each other with love in their eyes, even now. How lucky they were to have had fifty years together.

Leaving the hospital grounds, she was stopped in her tracks by a willowy blonde in figure-hugging red trousers and smart white linen jacket. 'Hi! Didn't we meet at the Bolton's barbecue recently?'

'Oh! Hallo. Yes, we did,' Camilla summoned up a smile. 'What are you doing here?'

'Meeting Ross, and I'm a bit late. He hates to be

kept waiting. Bye!' and Michaela hurried on her way.

So, it *was* as she had surmised. Michaela had obviously managed to resurrect their affair. And it must be to his liking, if his present frame of mind was anything to go by. Camilla sighed heavily. She wished with all her heart he had never come back to St Martin's. She wished their paths had never again been destined to cross and that he had remained a distant, if intriguing, memory.

Jean's wedding was set for twelve noon on the Saturday. Camilla felt suitably festive in her coral-pink outfit and straw boater. Arriving in good time, she met up with Matty who was in uniform, having slipped off the ward to attend the service.

They found seats about half-way down in the small ancient hospital chapel. It had been lavishly decorated for the occasion. Pedestals of summer flowers lit up the shadowy corners of the cool interior and there were golden lilies on the altar. Sunlight shafting through stained-glass windows fell across the old oak pews. There was a goodly sprinkling of staff among the congregation and the choir also was mostly composed of hospital personnel.

Smart in his grey morning dress, a white carnation in his buttonhole, the bridegroom was already seated in front with his best man. He was of average build with brown, neatly-styled straight hair and a healthy complexion.

'Have you ever met Duncan?' Matty murmured.

'No. Looks rather nice, doesn't he?' Camilla said.

She gazed around at the rest of the company, exchanging smiles with people she knew, listening to the lyrical recital with which the organist was filling the waiting moments.

Their own pew was not entirely full and presently Camilla looked up with a start to find Ross standing in the aisle alongside her.

'Can you make room for another one?' he murmured.

She smiled and moved along, thinking how heart-stoppingly handsome he looked in his morning dress.

The music had changed to the stirring strains of the Wedding March. The congregation rose as a radiant Jean arrived with her father to be conducted down the centre aisle by the minister. Elegant as always, she wore a stylish cream crêpe de Chine two-piece and a wide picture hat.

The words of the wedding service were always prone to bring a lump to Camilla's throat. *Will you love her, comfort her, honour her . . . forsaking all others . . . as long as you both shall live . . .* And she couldn't even get past the first verse of the chosen hymn 'Oh Perfect Love'. Ross's deep voice beside her, singing heartily, made it even more poignant. She blew her nose surreptitiously.

The service concluded, the bridal party moved into the vestry to sign the register. Ross leaned towards Camilla and whispered in her ear, 'Do you always cry at weddings?'

With a self-conscious grin she murmured back, 'It's the thought of another free spirit biting the dust, I expect.'

'Oh, Jean will be okay. I imagine she's got her priorities right.'

'And what do you think they should be?'

Stroking his firm chin, he eyed her wickedly. 'She promised to love, honour and obey. Sensible girl.'

'I don't know about sensible. I wouldn't agree to the obey bit.'

'Knowing you, that doesn't surprise me.'

'What makes you think you know me?' she said.

'Perhaps I know you better than you think.'

His challenging eyes meeting hers made her heart stampede. She glanced away, glad that at that moment the organ voluntary changed to triumphal music as bride and groom reappeared. Followed by members of their families, they made their joyful way down the aisle and out into the sunshine.

The rest of the company filed out after them and assembled for the official photographs. Private cameras also clicked. Camilla snapped away with hers, taking pictures of various groups including one of Ross. At least she would have a picture of him to look at sometimes when miles and years separated them.

People visiting patients in the hospital paused to stare, curious at the unusual spectacle of a wedding party mixed up with the normal traffic of the square—nurses, ancillary staff, white-coated medics and the like.

The photography over, Matty left to go back on duty while Camilla joined the other guests making their way over to the Great Hall and the reception. She had lost sight of Ross, but Ken and Lucy caught her up on the grand staircase at the top of which Jean waited to introduce Duncan to her friends. There were kisses and congratulations. Champagne flowed and laughter rang out.

In the Great Hall the portraits of past worthies gazed down on tables decorated with pink roses and a splendid three-tier wedding cake. When it was time to take their places, Camilla was glad to find herself sitting with Ken and Lucy along with one of the radiologists. Ross was further down on the other side of the table. She was relieved, yet sorry. Even though conversation with her immediate neighbours was lively and entertaining, she could not help her eyes straying in his direction. She wondered how long it would be before he and Michaela would be naming the day, if indeed he had changed his mind about marriage.

Making a determined effort not to spoil the occasion with depressing thoughts, she concentrated her attention on her companions.

The leisurely meal was punctuated by the reading of telegrams and speeches and toasts, after which Jean and her husband retired to a side room to change before leaving for the airport and their honeymoon.

Everyone crowded down to the square to wave them on their way amid a shower of confetti. They left with their car trailing beer cans and an old boot.

As always, when bride and groom had gone things seemed to fall a little flat. Camilla stood talking with Ken and Lucy for a while until Lucy said,

'Well, we'd better get going, Ken, or my folks will think we're not coming.'

Other people also were beginning to drift away. In her bag Camilla had the invitation from Dominic Bolton. She decided she might as well go along and see his exhibition at the gallery in Regent Street. Going back up the stairs to the Great Hall to take her leave of Jean's parents, she found herself joined by Ross.

Having said their goodbyes, they left the hall together. 'And what do you propose to do now?' he wanted to know.

'Me? I'm going to see Dominic Bolton's art exhibition.' She paused. 'Would you be interested in coming?' She didn't quite know what had prompted her to say that.

'No,' he said firmly, 'and you don't want to go either. Spending a lovely afternoon like this in some crummy art gallery? Ridiculous.'

Something in his manner made her catch her breath. She could only look at him, wide-eyed, wondering what was coming next.

'Anyway, you don't belong in his world,' he went on resolutely. 'Let's go for a drive. You and I have a lot of things to get straight.' Putting a possessive hand on her arm, he guided her across the square.

'I—I . . . wh-what things?' She felt breathless, having to quicken her steps to keep pace with his long stride.

He looked down at her steadily. 'Come *on*, Camilla. You don't need to ask.'

She had an odd presentiment that something unbelievable was about to happen. Her blood raced. But if it was what her instincts told her, then where did Michaela fit in?

'I—I wish you'd stop talking in riddles,' she said. 'What the hell are you on about?'

He laughed softly, took her hand and lead her towards the walkway in the direction of the Barbican. 'We'll go back to my flat so that I can get into something less formal. Then we can get down to business.'

'You do love being mysterious, don't you? As far as I'm aware, we've got nothing to discuss.'

His eyes were teasing. 'Oh yes we have.'

'The champagne must have gone to your head,' she said.

'I'm afraid it's something far more potent than champagne.'

She let out an exaggerated sigh. 'You're the most infuriating man I've ever met.'

'Well, I suppose that gives me some kind of distinction,' he returned, his lips twitching.

They had by now arrived at his flat. Her limbs developed an awful weakness as he put the key in the door. She had an impulse to turn and run but was powerless to do so.

Once inside he closed the door and began loosening his tie as he made for the bedroom. 'Make yourself at home, Camilla. I shan't be a minute . . .'

She took off her hat and went over to the window, gazing down at the lake and gardens below, trying to still her racing heart. She felt rather than heard him come back and turned to see him standing in the doorway. He had discarded his wedding clothes for an open-necked sports shirt and navy cords. Love welled up within her at the sight of him.

'Come here,' he said in a low voice, beckoning her.

She went, unable to help herself. He ran his fingers through her glowing hair before letting his hands come to rest on her shoulders. 'I've been wanting to do that for a long time.'

She almost stopped breathing. The physical contact through the thin silk of her dress was electrifying. Was he going to make love to her? Because if he was, she knew she could not resist him.

She said hesitantly: 'But . . . I thought . . . you didn't even like me . . . much.'

'I've tried very hard not to,' he admitted. 'It's been a losing battle. Camilla, you adorable girl,' he sighed, his eyes searching hers, 'I'm a hopeless case—a lovesick idiot. I've got all the classic symptoms. Palpitations when I see you, pain when I don't. Sleeplessness, inability to concentrate. A ridiculous aversion to other men paying you attention and a desire to kiss you when you flash your green eyes at me. Darling, I'm hooked. So there you are!'

'Oh, Ross!' Her arms reached out to him, she couldn't help it. 'Don't talk. Kiss me then.'

He did just that, and they clung together in a rapturous embrace. She was delirious with happiness. It was too wonderful to be true. But a small voice somewhere inside told her that there were things they did have to get straight before she succumbed to his powerful persuasion.

When his lips left hers for a moment, she drew a little away, saying in a shaky voice, 'Ross, I'm not living with you.'

He took her chin in his hand, a roguish gleam in his eyes. 'Not even when we're married?'

'But you said you weren't the marrying kind.'

'I'm also a selfish swine. I find I can't live without you.' His hand cupped her injured breast, caressing it gently. 'I discovered that when I thought you might be ill. I was absolutely stunned, my darling.'

She gave a guarded smile. 'I thought, the other night, that you were getting back together again with Michaela. You did meet her, didn't you?'

'How did you know that?'

'I saw her. She said hallo and told me.'

'Well, it was nothing that need concern you. She wanted my professional advice. I put her in touch with a guy I know.'

'Oh,' said Camilla with profound relief. 'I was

pea-green with envy. I thought . . . but how did you know I would feel the same way about you? I mean . . . we've had our differences, haven't we?'

'Call it intuition. Perhaps I saw what I wanted to see but didn't want to admit.' He drew her closer again, covering every inch of her face with kisses. 'You do realise . . . what you'll be taking on . . . don't you?' he murmured between endearments. 'It's no fun being married to a doctor. I'll be dragged from our bed in the middle of the night . . . there'll be endless demands on your patience . . .'

'I know, I know. And I don't care,' she said, her arms entwined around his neck. 'I'd rather have half your attention than none at all . . .'

He pressed his nose to hers. 'Then I think you had better take me down to Dorset at the first opportunity. And St Martin's had better prepare itself for another wedding.'

Holding her even closer, he sought her willing mouth again. The depths of his passion held her captive. She responded with all her being as his loving melted away any doubt.

And it was some time before they could bring themselves to take that drive in the country.

Have a romantic Christmas.

Roses, Always Roses
CLAUDIA JAMESON

Lady Surrender
CAROLE MORTIMER

Malibu Music
ROSEMARY HAMMOND

The Other Side of Paradise
MARGARET PARGETER

Put some more romance into your Christmas, with four brand new titles from Mills and Boon in one attractive gift pack.

They're all perfect reading for the holiday, and at only £4.40 it's easy to give the gift of romance.

Or better still, drop a hint that you'd like a little romance this Christmas.

Available from 11th October 1985 – look out for this gift pack where you buy Mills and Boon.